# On This Journey

Prayer Journal for Young People
Volume 2

# On This Journey

## Prayer Journal for Young People
## Volume 2

### By

### Rev. Onedia N. Gage

Books by

# Onedia N. Gage, Ph. D.

Are You Ready for 9th Grade . . . Again? A Family's Guide to Success
As We Grow Together Daily Devotional for Expectant Couples
As We Grow Together Prayer Journal for Expectant Couples
The Best 40 Days of Your Life: A Journey of Spiritual Renewal
The Blue Print: Poetry for the Soul
From Two to One: The Notebook for the Christian Couple
Hannah's Voice: Powerful Lessons in Prayer
Her Story: Bible Study
Her Story: Daily Devotional
Her Story: The Legacy of Her Fight
Her Story: The Legacy Journal
Her Story: Prayers and Journal
ILY! A Mother Daughter Success Kit
In Her Own Words: Notebook for the Christian Woman
In Purple Ink: Poetry for the Spirit
The Intensive Retreat for Couples for Her
The Intensive Retreat for Couples for Him
Living a Whole Life: Sermons which Promote, Prompt and Provoke Life
Love Letters to God from a Teenage Girl
The Measure of a Woman: The Details of Her Soul
The Notebook: For Me, About Me, By Me
The Notebook for the Christian Teen
On This Journey Daily Devotional for Young People
On This Journey Prayer Journal for Young People
On This Journey Daily Devotional for Young People, Vol 2
One Day More Than We Deserve Daily Devotional for the Growing Christian
One Day More Than We Deserve Prayer Journal for the Growing Christian
Promises, Promises: A Christian Novel
Queen in the Making: Girls Rites of Passage
Tools for These Times: Timely Sermons for Uncertain Times
With An Anointed Voice: The Power of Prayer
Yielded and Submitted: A Woman's Journey for a Life Dedicated to God
Yielded and Submitted: A Woman's Journey for a Life Dedicated to God Intimate Study
Yielded and Submitted: A Woman's Journey for a Life Dedicated to God Prayers and Journal

# Library of Congress

On This Journey
Prayer Journal for Young People
Volume 2

All Rights Reserved © 2016
by Onedia N. Gage

No part of this book may be reproduced or transmitted in any part of form or by any means, graphic, electronic or mechanical, including photocopying, recording, taping, or by any information storage of retrieval system, without the permission in writing from the publisher.

For information, please contact:
Purple Ink, Inc.
P O Box 300113
Houston, TX 77230
www.purpleink.net
onediagage@purpleink.net

**Onedia Gage Ministries**
www.onediagage.com
onediagage@onediagage.com

ISBN 978-1-939119-56-8

Printed in the United States

# What God Said

Be anxious for nothing, but in everything by prayer and supplication with thanksgiving let your requests be made to God.
**Philippians 4:6 NAS**

In the same way, the Spirit helps us in our weakness. We do not know what we ought to pray for, but the Spirit himself intercedes for us with groans that words cannot express.
**Romans 8:26 NIV**

Until now you have not asked for anything in my name. Ask and you will receive, and your joy will be complete.
**John 16:24 NIV**

# Dedication

Hillary Nicole, may these words guide and motivate you to be faithful to God and the path He has planned for you. Lean on Him and depend on Him for all of your needs. When I started this project, I didn't know you would be born before I was finished. I love you and will always be here for you.

Nehemiah Christian, may these words inspire you to honor God through who you are. God has great plans for you. I look forward to the great works He has planned for you and through you. You were born before we printed this, so I am excited to have you here. I love you and will always be here for you.

To our children—our gifts from God—If I pray for you, then you will remain strong.

To my prayer warriors, may all of our prayers be answered.

To the youth whose lives this will touch: may these words inspire you to respond to God's calling. Keep your relationship with God healthy. May these words inspire you to desire to achieve the level God has planned for you. My prayers are for you daily.

## Dear Hillary Nicole:

This is volume 2 of a beautiful prayer journal and time with God. We have a lot to pray for and to be thankful for. We have come this far by faith. We did not see any of this coming but it all arrived and for that we are grateful. When I put this together, I thought of our current journey and how we are whole again. This life is a journey and not all of it is smooth. We are going to be blessed according to God's riches and glory in Jesus Christ.

When I started writing this devotional in 1999, I had only dreamed of you—my little girl. I wrote this for you and now that you are here, I am so excited. I read and talk to you about God all the time. I pray over you every day. I love you and your healthy spiritual wellness is extremely important to me.

You will encounter things—all of which I may not mention specifically—for which I have prepared you. At that time, it may not seem as if I have but you are prepared and most importantly you are covered with my prayers and God's protection.

May the Lord bless you and keep you. May the light of His countenance shine on you and give you His peace. May He bless you as you go out and come in; rise early and settle late; in your labor and your leisure; in your laughter and in your tears.

I love you always!

Love,
*Mommy*
Onedia N. Gage

## Dear Nehemiah Christian:

When I finished this project and was ready to print, you were due. I was excited for you to finally be here. I read and talk to you about God all the time. I pray over you everyday. I love you and your healthy spiritual wellness is extremely important to me.

When you are old enough to read this, I urge you to ask as many questions as you need. I am right here for you as your example of Christianity and your biggest supporter.

You will encounter things —all of which I may not mention specifically—for which I have prepared you. At that time, it may not seem as if I have but you are prepared and most importantly you are covered with my prayers and God's protection.

May the Lord bless you and keep you. May the light of His countenance shine on you and give you His peace. May He bless you as you go out and come in; rise early and settle late; in your labor and your leisure; in your laughter and in your tears.

I love you always!

Love,
*Mommy*
Onedia N. Gage

**Dear Christian Teen:**

It is awesome you've selected *On This Journey Prayer Journal for Young People* for use as your personal journal. Your study of God's word is extremely important. Your intimate time with God is equally as important. *OTJ* will help you remain consistent with your time dedicated to God. I started on a journey with Christ at a very early age. I accepted Jesus as my Lord and Savior at age 8. Our journey has been one full of excitement and discovery. I have excited and disappointed God in my life. I have learned a lot, too.

Each day is dated such that you may start as soon as you receive your journal. Each day starts with a scripture and ends with a prayer. The space is for your expressions to God and what God is telling you. This is your time with God. Your intimacy level is affected by the quality time spent. This is not a diary but a prayer journal for the prayers you have, inclusive of your desires, petitions, pleas, and thanksgiving.

I wrote *OTJ* because biblical resources for youth are limited and young people need resources to succeed. As a young person, I struggled to find resources to help me with my walk with God. I didn't want my child or others to have the same trouble. *OTJ* allows you the freedom to express yourself to God and not limit yourself to answering questions. This journal is the personal documentation and will not resemble another's. Feel free to express yourself in anyway the Lord leads you. Keep a list of your prayers to God so that when He answers you will know He has answered you. Often, Christians assume that God has ignored us, but He has not forgotten our plea, nor our desires, not even our needs. We were the ones who forgot. God doesn't forget our prayers—not even the little ones.

You should expect to spend 30 minutes daily: 10 minutes to read and 20 minutes writing in your journal. You also need to make time to pray, which may last two minutes or ten minutes. You and God will determine that time. You also should expect to address your issues in a new and honest way. For example, you may not have known how to talk to God before but now you'll know better about your conversations with God. Your growth and maturity will demand a new attitude about God, His word, your commitment, inclusive of your study time, prayer life and lifestyle.

My prayer for you daily is that God blesses you beyond measure, cover you in His love and give you the desires of your heart. I also ask for your increased growth, maturity, knowledge and enlightenment through your increased study and commune with God. May you follow the direction and guidance of the Holy Spirit. I pray that God forgives you according to His word rather than what we deserve.

I pray that you are patient when God doesn't answer you when you want Him to. I pray He grant you favor when you encounter storms and uncertain times. I pray for grace for you when you don't understand God's work, will and plan. I pray for mercy for you when you question God and when we deserve worse than what He does. Overall, I pray God's continued anointing of you and your ventures. I pray that God's love continue to embrace you and motivate you to achieve your dreams. In your youthfulness and folly, I pray God forgive you for any youthful indiscretions. I also pray He show you how to forgive yourself for any mistakes you make.

Just a last note, 1 Thessalonians 5:17, Matthew 5:44 and Luke 6:28 are all scriptures which address prayer, its importance, and His expectations of prayer. When in doubt, seek His face. He will reveal Himself and answers you will never anticipate.

If you should need to reach me for questions, prayer or additional resources, please email me at onediagage@purpleink.net or onediagage@onediagage.com.

In Christ,

*Onedia Gage*

Onedia N. Gage

**Dear Parent:**

I just implore you as a parent to be attentive to your child, especially when they are highly inquisitive and precocious. Embrace their ideas and listen to them, even when you don't want to. They need your validation of who they are and whose they are. This validation stretches you in ways you may be unprepared to explore but without fear, I encourage your obedience as you approach the challenges your child presents. Your validity of them changes their life and strongly impacts their choices, leading them to what's right and away from what's wrong.

Life outside the parental box is far from easy. My short parenting journey thus far has proved interesting but doesn't make me and expert. Not even close. However, it does allow me to reflect on the type of child I was. Further, my childhood forces me to pray and ask my mother for forgiveness. Getting out of the box is required. First, abandoning the box means you are free to parent according to God's words. This means parenting with discipline and love and prayer, among other Christ-centered qualities and behaviors.

Secondly, the box is not good for neither parent nor child. Consider not parenting to please the society and your child rather than using God's word as your source for instruction. The Bible clearly defines the parental role. So is the child's. So the child cannot be in their role if you are not properly functioning within yours. Without the correct roles, friction, disobedience and discord results.

Lastly, the box presents a false sense of security and self-esteem. It also gives the illusion you have done the right thing. We compare our parenting to other parents rather than the Bible. This comparison gives a skewed snapshot of someone else's parental report card, if you will. The problem is that the next parents are presented with similar challenges as we ask them how they handled it then we decide what to do. This approach is disorderly. We are to ask God, refer to His Instructions and wait on His answer.

By the way, just because we made a better decision than another parent is not grounds for celebration. We need to pray for each other that we are able to present to strong, united, Christ-centered front. It is safe to discard the "box." God does not operate in that box. He does not want us in the box but will allow us in our time to discard the "box." Just a tip I learned from the wise woman who mothered me: 'so if she jumps off the bridge, are you going to jump, too?' I stopped using others to persuade my mother for things I wanted. Stop listening to what others do.

If you have any questions, are in need of prayer, or need more resources, please email me at onediagage@onediagage.com.

In Christ,

Onedia N. Gage

# TABLE OF CONTENTS

| | |
|---|---|
| Dedication | 11 |
| Letters | 13 |
| Why Prayer is Important | 22 |
| January | 23 |
| February | 54 |
| March | 83 |
| Developing Your Prayer Life—Part One | 114 |
| April | 115 |
| Writing Your Personal Testimony | 145 |
| May | 146 |
| June | 178 |
| Developing Your Prayer Life—Part Two | 207 |
| July | 208 |
| August | 239 |
| September | 270 |
| Reading God's Word | 300 |
| October | 301 |
| November | 332 |
| December | 362 |
| God's Answers to Your Prayers | 395 |
| Resources for the Journey | 397 |
| Index | 401 |
| Acknowledgements | 407 |
| About the Minister | 409 |

# WHY PRAYER IS IMPORTANT

Prayer is communication to God. Prayer is how we confess our sins and express our adoration, our fears, our desires, our needs, our everything to God. Prayer is one way God communicates with you, too. Prayer brings you to closer to God.

I Thessalonians 5:17 reads "pray continually." All the time. At every occasion. Prayer at meals is important, too as Jesus set forth that as important and led by example (John 6:11).

The following scriptures are about prayer: Matthew 5:44; 6:5-15; 26:36, 39-42; Luke 6:28; 18:1; 22:40; Romans 8:26; Mark 11:22-26; James 5:13-16; Philippians 4:6; and Ephesians 6:18-20.

These scriptures give instruction, encouragement and advice about prayer. Jesus is the leader of the movement and its importance. Jesus prayed to His Father for all occasions and is honest in His requests. God is true to His word and will hear and answer you.

Prayer can also be a period of praise and worship. Prayer is an integral instrument of your spiritual growth and maturity.

Prayer is critically important for your spiritual survival. Prayer feeds your spirit and fuels your soul.

Prayer Jornnal for Young People

# JANUARY 1

[26] Then God said, "Let Us make mankind in Our image, in Our likeness, so that they may rule over the fish in the sea and the birds in the sky, over the livestock and all the wild animals, and over all the creatures that move along the ground." [27] So God created mankind in His own image, in the image of God He created them; male and female He created them.

*Genesis 1:26-27*

_____
_____
_____
_____
_____
_____
_____
_____
_____
_____
_____
_____
_____
_____
_____
_____
_____
_____
_____
_____
_____
_____
_____
_____
_____

***Thank You, God, for creating me in Your image.***

# JANUARY 2

[28] God blessed them and said to them, "Be fruitful and increase in number; fill the earth and subdue it. Rule over the fish in the sea and the birds in the sky and over every living creature that moves on the ground." [29] Then God said, "I give you every seed-bearing plant on the face of the whole earth and every tree that has fruit with seed in it. They will be yours for food. [30] And to all the beasts of the earth and all the birds in the sky and all the creatures that move along the ground—everything that has the breath of life in it—I give every green plant for food." And it was so.

*Genesis 1:28-30*

*Lord, thank You for giving me a job.*

# JANUARY 3

[31] God saw all that He had made, and it was very good. And there was evening, and there was morning—the sixth day.

***Genesis 1:31***

*Lord, thank You for the privilege to call Your name.*

# JANUARY 4

Now, the serpent was more crafty than any of the wild animals the LORD God had made. He said to the woman, "Did God really say, 'You must not eat from any tree in the garden'?"

*Exodus 3:1*

*God, thank You for giving me direction.*

# JANUARY 5

⁶ When the woman saw that the fruit of the tree was good for food and pleasing to the eye, and also desirable for gaining wisdom, she took some and ate it. She also gave some to her husband, who was with her, and he ate it. ⁷ Then the eyes of both of them were opened, and they realized they were naked; so they sewed fig leaves together and made coverings for themselves.

***Genesis 3:6-7***

*Lord, please forgive me for my sins.*

# JANUARY 6

¹³ Then the LORD God said to the woman, "What is this you have done?" The woman said, "The serpent deceived me, and I ate."
¹⁴ So the LORD God said to the serpent, "Because you have done this, "Cursed are you above all livestock and all wild animals! You will crawl on your belly and you will eat dust all the days of your life.
¹⁵ And I will put enmity between you and the woman, and between your offspring and hers; he will crush your head, and you will strike his heel."
¹⁶ To the woman he said, "I will make your pains in childbearing very severe; with painful labor you will give birth to children. Your desire will be for your husband, and he will rule over you."

*Genesis 3:13-16*

*Lord, help me be on watch for those who intend to take my focus off of You.*

# JANUARY 7

[17] To Adam he said, "Because you listened to your wife and ate fruit from the tree about which I commanded you, 'You must not eat from it,' "Cursed is the ground because of you; through painful toil you will eat food from it all the days of your life.
[18] It will produce thorns and thistles for you, and you will eat the plants of the field.
[19] By the sweat of your brow you will eat your food until you return to the ground, since from it you were taken; for dust you are and to dust you will return."

*Genesis 3:17-19*

*Lord, I am sorry for the times when I disappoint You.*

# JANUARY 8

⁴ And Abel also brought an offering—fat portions from some of the firstborn of his flock. The LORD looked with favor on Abel and his offering, ⁵ but on Cain and his offering he did not look with favor. So Cain was very angry, and his face was downcast.
⁶ Then the LORD said to Cain, "Why are you angry? Why is your face downcast? ⁷ If you do what is right, will you not be accepted? But if you do not do what is right, sin is crouching at your door; it desires to have you, but you must rule over it."

*Genesis 4:4-7*

*Father, I really want Your favor.*

# JANUARY 9

⁸ Now Cain said to his brother Abel, "Let's go out to the field." While they were in the field, Cain attacked his brother Abel and killed him.
⁹ Then the LORD said to Cain, "Where is your brother Abel?"
"I don't know," he replied. "Am I my brother's keeper?"
¹⁰ The LORD said, "What have you done? Listen! Your brother's blood cries out to me from the ground. ¹¹ Now you are under a curse and driven from the ground, which opened its mouth to receive your brother's blood from your hand. ¹² When you work the ground, it will no longer yield its crops for you. You will be a restless wanderer on the earth."

*Genesis 4:8-12*

*Lord, help me be my brother's keeper. At all times.*

# JANUARY 10

[13] Cain said to the LORD, "My punishment is more than I can bear. [14] Today you are driving me from the land, and I will be hidden from your presence; I will be a restless wanderer on the earth, and whoever finds me will kill me." [15] But the LORD said to him, "Not so; anyone who kills Cain will suffer vengeance seven times over." Then the LORD put a mark on Cain so that no one who found him would kill him. [16] So Cain went out from the LORD's presence and lived in the land of Nod, east of Eden.

*Genesis 4:13-16*

*Thank You, Father for protecting me even though I do not deserve Your love.*

# JANUARY 11

[28] When Lamech had lived 182 years, he had a son. [29] He named him Noah and said, "He will comfort us in the labor and painful toil of our hands caused by the ground the LORD has cursed."

*Genesis 5*

*Lord, thank You for Your planning for me.*

# JANUARY 12

[3] Then the LORD said, "My Spirit will not contend with humans forever, for they are mortal; their days will be a hundred and twenty years."

*Genesis 6:3*

*Lord, I am apologetic that our disobedience causes You to change Your plans.*

# JANUARY 13

⁵ The LORD saw how great the wickedness of the human race had become on the earth, and that every inclination of the thoughts of the human heart was only evil all the time. ⁶ The LORD regretted that he had made human beings on the earth, and his heart was deeply troubled. ⁷ So the LORD said, "I will wipe from the face of the earth the human race I have created—and with them the animals, the birds and the creatures that move along the ground—for I regret that I have made them." ⁸ But Noah found favor in the eyes of the LORD.

*Genesis 6:5-8*

*Father, I hope that one day that I can find the type of favor that Noah experienced.*

# JANUARY 14

¹¹ Now the earth was corrupt in God's sight and was full of violence. ¹² God saw how corrupt the earth had become, for all the people on earth had corrupted their ways.

*Genesis 6:11-12*

*Lord, help me follow Your laws and decrees. I want to please You.*

Prayer Jornnal for Young People

# JANUARY 15

[13] So God said to Noah, "I am going to put an end to all people, for the earth is filled with violence because of them. I am surely going to destroy both them and the earth. [17] I am going to bring floodwaters on the earth to destroy all life under the heavens, every creature that has the breath of life in it. Everything on earth will perish.

*Genesis 6:13, 17*

*Lord, I never want You that angry again. Ever.*

MINISTER GAGE

# JANUARY 16

¹⁴ So make yourself an ark of cypress wood; make rooms in it and coat it with pitch inside and out. ¹⁵ This is how you are to build it: The ark is to be three hundred cubits long, fifty cubits wide and thirty cubits high. ¹⁶ Make a roof for it, leaving below the roof an opening one cubit high all around. Put a door in the side of the ark and make lower, middle and upper decks.

*Genesis 6:14-16*

*Lord, You are awesome and these dimensions just further serve as example.*

# JANUARY 17

[18] But I will establish my covenant with you, and you will enter the ark—you and your sons and your wife and your sons' wives with you. [19] You are to bring into the ark two of all living creatures, male and female, to keep them alive with you. [20] Two of every kind of bird, of every kind of animal and of every kind of creature that moves along the ground will come to you to be kept alive. [21] You are to take every kind of food that is to be eaten and store it away as food for you and for them."

*Genesis 6:18-21*

*Lord, thank You for Your covenant and everything that You promised me.*

# JANUARY 18

[22] Noah did everything just as God commanded him.

*Genesis 6:22*

*Lord, help me be still and to seek Your face.*

# JANUARY 19

¹¹ In the six hundredth year of Noah's life, on the seventeenth day of the second month—on that day all the springs of the great deep burst forth, and the floodgates of the heavens were opened. ¹² And rain fell on the earth forty days and forty nights.

*Genesis 7:11-12*

*Lord, You keep Your word and honor all of Your promises. Thank You for the ones You keep that You make to me.*

# JANUARY 20

[17] For forty days the flood kept coming on the earth, and as the waters increased they lifted the ark high above the earth. [18] The waters rose and increased greatly on the earth, and the ark floated on the surface of the water. [19] They rose greatly on the earth, and all the high mountains under the entire heavens were covered. [20] The waters rose and covered the mountains to a depth of more than fifteen cubits. [21] Every living thing that moved on land perished—birds, livestock, wild animals, all the creatures that swarm over the earth, and all mankind.

*Genesis 7:17-21*

**Lord, I Your wrath and hope for Your forgiveness in all things.**

# JANUARY 21

[22] Everything on dry land that had the breath of life in its nostrils died. [23] Every living thing on the face of the earth was wiped out; people and animals and the creatures that move along the ground and the birds were wiped from the earth. Only Noah was left, and those with him in the ark.

*Genesis 7:22-23*

**Lord, thank You for saving me from that wrath.**

# JANUARY 22

[24] The waters flooded the earth for a hundred and fifty days.

*Genesis 7:24*

*Lord, You caused rain for 6 months and rebuilt Your work with power. Lord, I love You.*

# JANUARY 23

[21] The LORD smelled the pleasing aroma and said in his heart: "Never again will I curse the ground because of humans, even though every inclination of the human heart is evil from childhood. And never again will I destroy all living creatures, as I have done.

*Genesis 8:21*

*Father, thank You for Your promise.*

# JANUARY 24

[12] And God said, "This is the sign of the covenant I am making between Me and you and every living creature with you, a covenant for all generations to come: [13] I have set My rainbow in the clouds, and it will be the sign of the covenant between Me and the earth. [14] Whenever I bring clouds over the earth and the rainbow appears in the clouds, [15] I will remember My covenant between Me and you and all living creatures of every kind. Never again will the waters become a flood to destroy all life. [16] Whenever the rainbow appears in the clouds, I will see it and remember the everlasting covenant between God and all living creatures of every kind on the earth."
[17] So God said to Noah, "This is the sign of the covenant I have established between Me and all life on the earth."

*Genesis 9:12-17*

*God, thank You for Your covenant, protection and promises.*

# JANUARY 25

[1]After this, the word of the LORD came to Abram in a vision:
"Do not be afraid, Abram.
   I am your shield,
   your very great reward."

*Genesis 15:1*

---

*Master, I come humbly thanking for Your Shield and Protection.*

# JANUARY 26

⁶ Abram believed the LORD, and he credited it to Him as righteousness.

***Genesis 15:6***

***Father, my belief in You waivers inexcusably and for that I apologize.***

# JANUARY 27

³ Now Israel loved Joseph more than any of his other sons, because he had been born to him in his old age; and he made an ornate robe for him. ⁴ When his brothers saw that their father loved him more than any of them, they hated him and could not speak a kind word to him.

*Genesis 37:3-4*

*Master, thanks for the parent—child love.*

# JANUARY 28

⁵ Joseph had a dream, and when he told it to his brothers, they hated him all the more. ⁶ He said to them, "Listen to this dream I had: ⁷ We were binding sheaves of grain out in the field when suddenly my sheaf rose and stood upright, while your sheaves gathered around mine and bowed down to it." ⁸ His brothers said to him, "Do you intend to reign over us? Will you actually rule us?" And they hated him all the more because of his dream and what he had said.

*Genesis 37:5-8*

*Lord, my God, thank You for discernment.*

# JANUARY 29

⁹ Then he had another dream, and he told it to his brothers. "Listen," he said, "I had another dream, and this time the sun and moon and eleven stars were bowing down to me." ¹⁰ When he told his father as well as his brothers, his father rebuked him and said, "What is this dream you had? Will your mother and I and your brothers actually come and bow down to the ground before you?"

*Genesis 37:9-10*

*Father, thank You for Your revelations.*

# JANUARY 30

[11] His brothers were jealous of him, but his father kept the matter in mind.

*Genesis 37:11*

*God, thank You for love and understanding.*

# JANUARY 31

[18] But they saw him in the distance, and before he reached them, they plotted to kill him.
[19] "Here comes that dreamer!" they said to each other. [20] "Come now, let's kill him and throw him into one of these cisterns and say that a ferocious animal devoured him. Then we'll see what comes of his dreams."
[21] When Reuben heard this, he tried to rescue him from their hands. "Let's not take his life," he said. [22] "Don't shed any blood. Throw him into this cistern here in the wilderness, but don't lay a hand on him." Reuben said this to rescue him from them and take him back to his father.

*Genesis 37:18-22*

*Father, thank You for Your grace and mercy.*

# FEBRUARY 1

²³ So when Joseph came to his brothers, they stripped him of his robe—the ornate robe he was wearing— ²⁴ and they took him and threw him into the cistern. The cistern was empty; there was no water in it. ²⁵ As they sat down to eat their meal, they looked up and saw a caravan of Ishmaelites coming from Gilead. Their camels were loaded with spices, balm and myrrh, and they were on their way to take them down to Egypt.

*Genesis 37:23-25*

_____
_____
_____
_____
_____
_____
_____
_____
_____
_____
_____
_____
_____
_____
_____
_____
_____
_____
_____
_____
_____
_____
_____
_____
_____
_____
_____
_____

*Father, thank You for Your Hand of protection.*

# FEBRUARY 2

²⁶ Judah said to his brothers, "What will we gain if we kill our brother and cover up his blood? ²⁷ Come, let's sell him to the Ishmaelites and not lay our hands on him; after all, he is our brother, our own flesh and blood." His brothers agreed. ²⁸ So when the Midianite merchants came by, his brothers pulled Joseph up out of the cistern and sold him for twenty shekels of silver to the Ishmaelites, who took him to Egypt. ²⁹ When Reuben returned to the cistern and saw that Joseph was not there, he tore his clothes.

*Exodus 37:26-29*

*Master, all of my strength and help comes from You. I am blessed.*

# FEBRUARY 3

²²ᵇ Reuben said this to rescue him from them and take him back to his father. ²⁹ When Reuben returned to the cistern and saw that Joseph was not there, he tore his clothes. ³⁰ He went back to his brothers and said, "The boy isn't there! Where can I turn now?"

*Genesis 37:22b, 29-30*

*Lord, thank You for those who are there to rescue me.*

# FEBRUARY 4

³¹ Then they got Joseph's robe, slaughtered a goat and dipped the robe in the blood. ³² They took the ornate robe back to their father and said, "We found this. Examine it to see whether it is your son's robe." ³³ He recognized it and said, "It is my son's robe! Some ferocious animal has devoured him. Joseph has surely been torn to pieces."

*Genesis 37:31-33*

*Lord, do not let me fall captive to my own family and friends.*

# FEBRUARY 5

³⁴ Then Jacob tore his clothes, put on sackcloth and mourned for his son many days. ³⁵ All his sons and daughters came to comfort him, but he refused to be comforted. "No," he said, "I will continue to mourn until I join my son in the grave." So his father wept for him.

*Genesis 37:34-35*

*Father, let me have that much compassion for my family.*

# FEBRUARY 6

³⁶ Meanwhile, the Midianites sold Joseph in Egypt to Potiphar, one of Pharaoh's officials, the captain of the guard. ¹ Now Joseph had been taken down to Egypt. Potiphar, an Egyptian who was one of Pharaoh's officials, the captain of the guard, bought him from the Ishmaelites who had taken him there.

*Genesis 37:36; 39:1*

*Father, watch over me when I am in foreign lands and at the mercy of strangers.*

# FEBRUARY 7

² The LORD was with Joseph so that he prospered, and he lived in the house of his Egyptian master. ³ When his master saw that the LORD was with him and that the LORD gave him success in everything he did, ⁴ Joseph found favor in his eyes and became his attendant. Potiphar put him in charge of his household, and he entrusted to his care everything he owned.

*Genesis 39:2-4*

*Lord, thank You for revealing to me that others see Your favor upon me, which influences them to have favor also.*

# FEBRUARY 8

⁵ From the time he put him in charge of his household and of all that he owned, the LORD blessed the household of the Egyptian because of Joseph. The blessing of the LORD was on everything Potiphar had, both in the house and in the field. ⁶ So Potiphar left everything he had in Joseph's care; with Joseph in charge, he did not concern himself with anything except the food he ate.

***Genesis 39:5-6***

*Lord, thank You for blessing those around me because of me.*

# FEBRUARY 9

Now Joseph was well-built and handsome, [7] and after a while his master's wife took notice of Joseph and said, "Come to bed with me!" [8] But he refused. "With me in charge," he told her, "my master does not concern himself with anything in the house; everything he owns he has entrusted to my care. [9] No one is greater in this house than I am. My master has withheld nothing from me except you, because you are his wife. How then could I do such a wicked thing and sin against God?" [10] And though she spoke to Joseph day after day, he refused to go to bed with her or even be with her.

*Genesis 39:6b-10*

*Lord, help me always maintain my integrity because I want to represent You well.*

# FEBRUARY 10

¹¹ One day he went into the house to attend to his duties, and none of the household servants was inside. ¹² She caught him by his cloak and said, "Come to bed with me!" But he left his cloak in her hand and ran out of the house. ¹³ When she saw that he had left his cloak in her hand and had run out of the house, ¹⁴ she called her household servants. "Look," she said to them, "this Hebrew has been brought to us to make sport of us! He came in here to sleep with me, but I screamed. ¹⁵ When he heard me scream for help, he left his cloak beside me and ran out of the house."

*Genesis 39:11-15*

*Lord, even when I am innocent, others will blame me. Keep me focused.*

# FEBRUARY 11

[20] Joseph's master took him and put him in prison, the place where the king's prisoners were confined. But while Joseph was there in the prison, [21] the LORD was with him; he showed him kindness and granted him favor in the eyes of the prison warden. [22] So the warden put Joseph in charge of all those held in the prison, and he was made responsible for all that was done there. [23] The warden paid no attention to anything under Joseph's care, because the LORD was with Joseph and gave him success in whatever he did.

*Genesis 39:20-23*

*Lord, thank You for the success in whatever I do.*

# FEBRUARY 12

[8] "We both had dreams," they answered, "but there is no one to interpret them." Then Joseph said to them, "Do not interpretations belong to God? Tell me your dreams."

***Genesis 40***

*Master, thank You for allowing me to escape stupidity.*

# FEBRUARY 13

[14] So Pharaoh sent for Joseph, and he was quickly brought from the dungeon. When he had shaved and changed his clothes, he came before Pharaoh. [15] Pharaoh said to Joseph, "I had a dream, and no one can interpret it. But I have heard it said of you that when you hear a dream you can interpret it." [16] "I cannot do it," Joseph replied to Pharaoh, "but God will give Pharaoh the answer he desires."

*Genesis 41:14-16*

*Lord, I will remember to give You credit for Your work.*

# FEBRUARY 14

[28] "It is just as I said to Pharaoh: God has shown Pharaoh what he is about to do. [29] Seven years of great abundance are coming throughout the land of Egypt, [30] but seven years of famine will follow them. Then all the abundance in Egypt will be forgotten, and the famine will ravage the land. [31] The abundance in the land will not be remembered, because the famine that follows it will be so severe. [32] The reason the dream was given to Pharaoh in two forms is that the matter has been firmly decided by God, and God will do it soon.

*Genesis 41:28-32*

*Lord, Your decisiveness and decisions need to be respected. I will.*

# FEBRUARY 15

[37] The plan seemed good to Pharaoh and to all his officials. [38] So Pharaoh asked them, "Can we find anyone like this man, one in whom is the spirit of God?" [39] Then Pharaoh said to Joseph, "Since God has made all this known to you, there is no one so discerning and wise as you. [40] You shall be in charge of my palace, and all my people are to submit to your orders. Only with respect to the throne will I be greater than you."

*Genesis 41:37-40*

*Lord, thank You for restoration and respect.*

# FEBRUARY 16

[41] So Pharaoh said to Joseph, "I hereby put you in charge of the whole land of Egypt." [42] Then Pharaoh took his signet ring from his finger and put it on Joseph's finger. He dressed him in robes of fine linen and put a gold chain around his neck. [43] He had him ride in a chariot as his second-in-command, and people shouted before him, "Make way!" Thus he put him in charge of the whole land of Egypt.

*Genesis 41:41-43*

*Lord, thank You for answering my prayers.*

# FEBRUARY 17

⁴⁶ Joseph was thirty years old when he entered the service of Pharaoh king of Egypt. And Joseph went out from Pharaoh's presence and traveled throughout Egypt.

***Genesis 41:46***

***Lord, thank You for using me in Your kingdom, for Your glory.***

# FEBRUARY 18

[47] During the seven years of abundance the land produced plentifully. [48] Joseph collected all the food produced in those seven years of abundance in Egypt and stored it in the cities. In each city he put the food grown in the fields surrounding it. [49] Joseph stored up huge quantities of grain, like the sand of the sea; it was so much that he stopped keeping records because it was beyond measure.

*Genesis 41:47-49*

*Lord, thank You for the wisdom to use the information You give to take action.*

# FEBRUARY 19

[50] Before the years of famine came, two sons were born to Joseph by Asenath daughter of Potiphera, priest of On. [51] Joseph named his firstborn Manasseh and said, "It is because God has made me forget all my trouble and all my father's household." [52] The second son he named Ephraim and said, "It is because God has made me fruitful in the land of my suffering."

*Genesis 41:50-52*

*God, thank You for blessing me when I was supposed to be suffering.*

# FEBRUARY 20

[53] The seven years of abundance in Egypt came to an end, [54] and the seven years of famine began, just as Joseph had said. There was famine in all the other lands, but in the whole land of Egypt there was food. [55] When all Egypt began to feel the famine, the people cried to Pharaoh for food. Then Pharaoh told all the Egyptians, "Go to Joseph and do what he tells you."

*Genesis 41:53-55*

*God, thank You for preparing me to do Your will and Your work.*

# FEBRUARY 21

¹When Jacob learned that there was grain in Egypt, he said to his sons, "Why do you just keep looking at each other?" ² He continued, "I have heard that there is grain in Egypt. Go down there and buy some for us, so that we may live and not die."

*Genesis 42:1-2*

**Lord, thank You for reminding me to work—taking action.**

# FEBRUARY 22

[3] Then ten of Joseph's brothers went down to buy grain from Egypt. [4] But Jacob did not send Benjamin, Joseph's brother, with the others, because he was afraid that harm might come to him. [5] So Israel's sons were among those who went to buy grain, for there was famine in the land of Canaan also. [6] Now Joseph was the governor of the land, the person who sold grain to all its people. So when Joseph's brothers arrived, they bowed down to him with their faces to the ground.

*Genesis 42:3-6*

*Lord, thank You for making Your will plain to me.*

# FEBRUARY 23

[7] As soon as Joseph saw his brothers, he recognized them, but he pretended to be a stranger and spoke harshly to them. "Where do you come from?" he asked. "From the land of Canaan," they replied, "to buy food." [8] Although Joseph recognized his brothers, they did not recognize him. [9] Then he remembered his dreams about them and said to them, "You are spies! You have come to see where our land is unprotected."

*Genesis 42:7-9*

*Lord, thank You for calling Your words and vision to my recollection and memory.*

# FEBRUARY 24

[18] On the third day, Joseph said to them, "Do this and you will live, for I fear God: [19] If you are honest men, let one of your brothers stay here in prison, while the rest of you go and take grain back for your starving households. [20] But you must bring your youngest brother to me, so that your words may be verified and that you may not die." This they proceeded to do.

*Genesis 42:18-20*

*Lord, thank You for being able to love and forgive others.*

# FEBRUARY 25

[21] They said to one another, "Surely we are being punished because of our brother. We saw how distressed he was when he pleaded with us for his life, but we would not listen; that's why this distress has come on us."

*Genesis 42:21*

*Father, thank You for revealing when I have hurt others so that I can repent.*

# FEBRUARY 26

[22] Reuben replied, "Didn't I tell you not to sin against the boy? But you wouldn't listen! Now we must give an accounting for his blood." [23] They did not realize that Joseph could understand them, since he was using an interpreter.

*Genesis 42:22-23*

*Father, thank You for holding me accountable and others as well.*

# FEBRUARY 27

²⁴ He turned away from them and began to weep, but then came back and spoke to them again. He had Simeon taken from them and bound before their eyes.

*Genesis 42:24*

*Father, thank You for keeping my heart soft and pliable.*

# FEBRUARY 28

[25] Joseph gave orders to fill their bags with grain, to put each man's silver back in his sack, and to give them provisions for their journey. After this was done for them, [26] they loaded their grain on their donkeys and left.

*Genesis 42:25-26*

*Father, thank You being able to keep Your word.*

# FEBRUARY 29

²⁷ At the place where they stopped for the night one of them opened his sack to get feed for his donkey, and he saw his silver in the mouth of his sack. ²⁸ "My silver has been returned," he said to his brothers. "Here it is in my sack." Their hearts sank and they turned to each other trembling and said, "What is this that God has done to us?" ²⁹ When they came to their father Jacob in the land of Canaan, they told him all that had happened to them..

*Genesis 42:27-29*

*Lord, thank You for blessing me when I am the least deserving.*

# MARCH 1

They said, [30] "The man who is lord over the land spoke harshly to us and treated us as though we were spying on the land. [31] But we said to him, 'We are honest men; we are not spies. [32] We were twelve brothers, sons of one father. One is no more, and the youngest is now with our father in Canaan.' [33] "Then the man who is lord over the land said to us, 'This is how I will know whether you are honest men: Leave one of your brothers here with me, and take food for your starving households and go. [34] But bring your youngest brother to me so I will know that you are not spies but honest men. Then I will give your brother back to you, and you can trade in the land.'"

*Genesis 42:30-34*

*Master, thank You for sharing with me the blessings from others because of You.*

# MARCH 2

[35] As they were emptying their sacks, there in each man's sack was his pouch of silver! When they and their father saw the money pouches, they were frightened.

*Genesis 42:35*

*Lord, thank You for the gifts.*

# MARCH 3

[36] Their father Jacob said to them, "You have deprived me of my children. Joseph is no more and Simeon is no more, and now you want to take Benjamin. Everything is against me!"

*Genesis 42:36*

*Lord God, please do not hold everything against me.*

# MARCH 4

[37] Then Reuben said to his father, "You may put both of my sons to death if I do not bring him back to you. Entrust him to my care, and I will bring him back."
[38] But Jacob said, "My son will not go down there with you; his brother is dead and he is the only one left. If harm comes to him on the journey you are taking, you will bring my gray head down to the grave in sorrow."

*Genesis 42:37-38*

*Thank you, Father for trusting me.*

# MARCH 5

⁶ Israel asked, "Why did you bring this trouble on me by telling the man you had another brother?" ⁷ They replied, "The man questioned us closely about ourselves and our family. 'Is your father still living?' he asked us. 'Do you have another brother?' We simply answered his questions. How were we to know he would say, 'Bring your brother down here'?"

*Genesis 43:6-7*

**Lord God, thank You for Your honesty.**

# MARCH 6

⁸ Then Judah said to Israel his father, "Send the boy along with me and we will go at once, so that we and you and our children may live and not die. ⁹ I myself will guarantee his safety; you can hold me personally responsible for him. If I do not bring him back to you and set him here before you, I will bear the blame before you all my life. ¹⁰ As it is, if we had not delayed, we could have gone and returned twice."

*Genesis 43:8-10*

_____
_____
_____
_____
_____
_____
_____
_____
_____
_____
_____
_____
_____
_____
_____
_____
_____
_____
_____
_____
_____
_____
_____
_____
_____
_____
_____

*Father, thank You for allowing me to participate in Your work.*

# MARCH 7

[11] Then their father Israel said to them, "If it must be, then do this: Put some of the best products of the land in your bags and take them down to the man as a gift—a little balm and a little honey, some spices and myrrh, some pistachio nuts and almonds. [12] Take double the amount of silver with you, for you must return the silver that was put back into the mouths of your sacks. Perhaps it was a mistake. [13] Take your brother also and go back to the man at once. [14] And may God Almighty grant you mercy before the man so that he will let your other brother and Benjamin come back with you. As for me, if I am bereaved, I am bereaved."

*Genesis 43:11-14*

*Lord, thank You for molding and forming me. For I am Your piece of work.*

# MARCH 8

[15] So the men took the gifts and double the amount of silver, and Benjamin also. They hurried down to Egypt and presented themselves to Joseph. [16] When Joseph saw Benjamin with them, he said to the steward of his house, "Take these men to my house, slaughter an animal and prepare a meal; they are to eat with me at noon."

*Genesis 43:15-16*

*Father, thank You for the example of hospitality.*

# MARCH 9

[19] So they went up to Joseph's steward and spoke to him at the entrance to the house. [20] "We beg your pardon, our lord," they said, "we came down here the first time to buy food. [21] But at the place where we stopped for the night we opened our sacks and each of us found his silver—the exact weight—in the mouth of his sack. So we have brought it back with us. [22] We have also brought additional silver with us to buy food. We don't know who put our silver in our sacks."

*Genesis 43:19-22*

*Thank You God for giving me favor.*

# MARCH 10

[23] "It's all right," he said. "Don't be afraid. Your God, the God of your father, has given you treasure in your sacks; I received your silver." Then he brought Simeon out to them.

*Genesis 43:23*

_____
_____
_____
_____
_____
_____
_____
_____
_____
_____
_____
_____
_____
_____
_____
_____
_____
_____
_____
_____
_____
_____
_____
_____
_____
_____
_____
_____
_____
_____

*Thank You Lord for others having favor with me.*

# MARCH 11

[24] The steward took the men into Joseph's house, gave them water to wash their feet and provided fodder for their donkeys. [25] They prepared their gifts for Joseph's arrival at noon, because they had heard that they were to eat there. [26] When Joseph came home, they presented to him the gifts they had brought into the house, and they bowed down before him to the ground. [27] He asked them how they were, and then he said, "How is your aged father you told me about? Is he still living?" [28] They replied, "Your servant our father is still alive and well." And they bowed down, prostrating themselves before him.

*Genesis 43:24-28*

*Thank You, Lord, for the people who care for and take care of me.*

# MARCH 12

[29] As he looked about and saw his brother Benjamin, his own mother's son, he asked, "Is this your youngest brother, the one you told me about?" And he said, "God be gracious to you, my son." [30] Deeply moved at the sight of his brother, Joseph hurried out and looked for a place to weep. He went into his private room and wept there. [31] After he had washed his face, he came out and, controlling himself, said, "Serve the food."

*Genesis 29-31*

*Thank You, Lord, for what You do to bring love to me.*

# MARCH 13

³² They served him by himself, the brothers by themselves, and the Egyptians who ate with him by themselves, because Egyptians could not eat with Hebrews, for that is detestable to Egyptians. ³³ The men had been seated before him in the order of their ages, from the firstborn to the youngest; and they looked at each other in astonishment. ³⁴ When portions were served to them from Joseph's table, Benjamin's portion was five times as much as anyone else's. So they feasted and drank freely with him.

*Genesis 43:32-34*

*Thank You, Lord for Your riches being bestowed on me.*

# MARCH 14

¹ Now Joseph gave these instructions to the steward of his house: "Fill the men's sacks with as much food as they can carry, and put each man's silver in the mouth of his sack. ² Then put my cup, the silver one, in the mouth of the youngest one's sack, along with the silver for his grain." And he did as Joseph said.

*Genesis 44:1-2*

*Father, thank You for blessings that You so graciously bestow on me.*

# MARCH 15

¹¹ Each of them quickly lowered his sack to the ground and opened it. ¹² Then the steward proceeded to search, beginning with the oldest and ending with the youngest. And the cup was found in Benjamin's sack. ¹³ At this, they tore their clothes. Then they all loaded their donkeys and returned to the city.

*Genesis 44:11-13*

*Father, forgive me for what I do which harms Your name.*

# MARCH 16

[17] But Joseph said, "Far be it from me to do such a thing! Only the man who was found to have the cup will become my slave. The rest of you, go back to your father in peace."

*Genesis 44:17*

*Father, let me not question You when You do what You will.*

# MARCH 17

[30] "So now, if the boy is not with us when I go back to your servant my father, and if my father, whose life is closely bound up with the boy's life, [31] sees that the boy isn't there, he will die. Your servants will bring the gray head of our father down to the grave in sorrow. [32] Your servant guaranteed the boy's safety to my father. I said, 'If I do not bring him back to you, I will bear the blame before you, my father, all my life!' [33] "Now then, please let your servant remain here as my lord's slave in place of the boy, and let the boy return with his brothers. [34] How can I go back to my father if the boy is not with me? No! Do not let me see the misery that would come on my father."

*Genesis 44:18-34*

*Father, help me share my testimony so that others will be blessed and be compassionate to me.*

# MARCH 18

[1] Then Joseph could no longer control himself before all his attendants, and he cried out, "Have everyone leave my presence!" So there was no one with Joseph when he made himself known to his brothers. [2] And he wept so loudly that the Egyptians heard him, and Pharaoh's household heard about it.

*Genesis 45:1-2*

___

*Father, thank You for keeping me humble and compassionate. Thank You for moving on my heart.*

# MARCH 19

[3] Joseph said to his brothers, "I am Joseph! Is my father still living?" But his brothers were not able to answer him, because they were terrified at his presence.
[4] Then Joseph said to his brothers, "Come close to me." When they had done so, he said, "I am your brother Joseph, the one you sold into Egypt!

*Genesis 45:3-4*

*God, thank You for allowing me to forgive, love and confess.*

# MARCH 20

[5] And now, do not be distressed and do not be angry with yourselves for selling me here, because it was to save lives that God sent me ahead of you.

*Genesis 45:5*

*Lord, thank You for letting me see and participate in Your will and Your work.*

# MARCH 21

⁶ For two years now there has been famine in the land, and for the next five years there will be no plowing and reaping. ⁷ But God sent me ahead of you to preserve for you a remnant on earth and to save your lives by a great deliverance.

*Genesis 45:6-7*

**Lord, thank You for my humbleness which leads to sharing with others.**

# MARCH 22

⁸ "So then, it was not you who sent me here, but God. He made me father to Pharaoh, lord of his entire household and ruler of all Egypt. ⁹ Now hurry back to my father and say to him, 'This is what your son Joseph says: God has made me lord of all Egypt. Come down to me; don't delay. ¹⁰ You shall live in the region of Goshen and be near me—you, your children and grandchildren, your flocks and herds, and all you have. ¹¹ I will provide for you there, because five years of famine are still to come. Otherwise you and your household and all who belong to you will become destitute.'

*Genesis 45:8-11*

*Lord, thank You for making me a provider for others.*

# MARCH 23

[12] "You can see for yourselves, and so can my brother Benjamin, that it is really I who am speaking to you. [13] Tell my father about all the honor accorded me in Egypt and about everything you have seen. And bring my father down here quickly."

*Genesis 45:12-13*

*Father, when You make a statement, You are so profound—causing shock and awe.*

# MARCH 24

[14] Then he threw his arms around his brother Benjamin and wept, and Benjamin embraced him, weeping. [15] And he kissed all his brothers and wept over them. Afterward his brothers talked with him.

*Genesis 45:14-15*

*Father, thank You for loving me and equipping me to love others, even when they have abused me.*

# MARCH 25

[16] When the news reached Pharaoh's palace that Joseph's brothers had come, Pharaoh and all his officials were pleased. [17] Pharaoh said to Joseph, "Tell your brothers, 'Do this: Load your animals and return to the land of Canaan, [18] and bring your father and your families back to me. I will give you the best of the land of Egypt and you can enjoy the fat of the land.'"
[19] "You are also directed to tell them, 'Do this: Take some carts from Egypt for your children and your wives, and get your father and come. [20] Never mind about your belongings, because the best of all Egypt will be yours.'"

*Genesis 45:16-20*

*Lord, thank You for a place to call home and somewhere where I can welcome others to do the same.*

# MARCH 26

[24] Then he sent his brothers away, and as they were leaving he said to them, "Don't quarrel on the way!"

*Genesis 45:24*

*Lord, thank You for sharing Your gift of wisdom with me .*

# MARCH 27

[26] They told him, "Joseph is still alive! In fact, he is ruler of all Egypt." Jacob was stunned; he did not believe them. [27] But when they told him everything Joseph had said to them, and when he saw the carts Joseph had sent to carry him back, the spirit of their father Jacob revived. [28] And Israel said, "I'm convinced! My son Joseph is still alive. I will go and see him before I die."

***Genesis 45:26-28***

*God, thank You for giving me something to celebrate after such a long time of sorrow. Thank You for answering my prayers.*

# MARCH 28

¹ So Israel set out with all that was his, and when he reached Beersheba, he offered sacrifices to the God of his father Isaac. ² And God spoke to Israel in a vision at night and said, "Jacob! Jacob!" "Here I am," he replied. ³ "I am God, the God of your father," he said. "Do not be afraid to go down to Egypt, for I will make you into a great nation there. ⁴ I will go down to Egypt with you, and I will surely bring you back again. And Joseph's own hand will close your eyes."

*Genesis 46:1-4*

*Master, thank You for Your voice and direction and exposure to Your wisdom.*

# MARCH 29

[26] All those who went to Egypt with Jacob—those who were his direct descendants, not counting his sons' wives—numbered sixty-six persons. [27] With the two sons who had been born to Joseph in Egypt, the members of Jacob's family, which went to Egypt, were seventy in all.

*Genesis 46:5-27*

*Lord, thank You for allowing me to be a part of such a powerful legacy.*

# MARCH 30

²⁹ Joseph had his chariot made ready and went to Goshen to meet his father Israel. As soon as Joseph appeared before him, he threw his arms around his father and wept for a long time.

*****Genesis 46:29*****

*Oh Lord, thank You for the steward to whom I am assigned. May I be ever grateful to have a steward—without complaint.*

# MARCH 31

[30] Israel said to Joseph, "Now I am ready to die, since I have seen for myself that you are still alive."

***Genesis 46:30***

*Lord, I surrender all that I am to You.*

# DEVELOPING YOUR PRAYER LIFE— PART ONE

## *What is Prayer?*

Prayer is your conversation to God and God's conversation to you. Prayer includes adoration, confession, thanksgiving, and supplication.

Each prayer will not be the same and will never include the same content. There is no "correct" prayer, so that means there is no "incorrect" prayer either. Prayer is your time to communicate and commune with God. There is no specific length of time to pray.

Prayer requires a few things though. Prayer requires desire to communicate with God. It also requires an honest approach to God. Prayer requires your initiative. Prayer does not require fancy words (Biblical vernacular) or the prayers of others.

Prayer can be intimidating. When your elders pray, you may think 'I want to pray like ___ _____.' You complete the blank, but God doesn't require that. Try to avoid being intimidated by prayer. God just wants your pure heart and your honesty.

Let's start with how to approach God. Your approach should be of reverence. We are first taught to bow our heads and close our eyes. Our posture for prayer should be respectful to God. Does this rule out praying and driving? No, because my heart is humbled and bowed, and my spirit desires me to pray to God. Often times your environment needs to be changed in order to offer Him your full respect and attention.

Your words. What do I say to God? I want Him to know I love Him. I want Him to know how grateful I am to Him for waking me up. I am really glad He healed my grandmother. I am really sorry I cheated on my test at school. All of these statements can be said to God just as they are and they can be said individually or collectively. These statements need not be dressed or nor added to.

Later, as you mature as a Christian, more content will be added to your prayer time. You will be able to release everything to God. Sometimes you will share with God almost immediately. Your prayer life means that you pray regularly and fervently (with intimacy and communion). You have started to develop your prayer life when prayer comes to your mind and heart without an outside reminder. You will also yearn to share with God. Your time with God becomes more and more important. This intimacy with God will grow the more time you spend with Him.

There will come to pass a day when someone will ask you to pray. This invitation then confirms your prayer life is active. If the invitation never happens, then you offer to pray—another signal that your prayer life is active.

# APRIL 1

¹ Joseph went and told Pharaoh, "My father and brothers, with their flocks and herds and everything they own, have come from the land of Canaan and are now in Goshen." ² He chose five of his brothers and presented them before Pharaoh. ³ Pharaoh asked the brothers, "What is your occupation?" "Your servants are shepherds," they replied to Pharaoh, "just as our fathers were." ⁴ They also said to him, "We have come to live here for a while, because the famine is severe in Canaan and your servants' flocks have no pasture. So now, please let your servants settle in Goshen."

*Genesis 47*

*Father, when I lead may I remain humble and focused on You!*

# APRIL 2

[15] Then he blessed Joseph and said, "May the God before whom my fathers Abraham and Isaac walked faithfully, the God who has been my shepherd all my life to this day,
[16] the Angel[A.l] who has delivered me from all harm—may he bless these boys. May they be called by my name and the names of my fathers Abraham and Isaac, and may they increase greatly on the earth." [17] When Joseph saw his father placing his right hand on Ephraim's head he was displeased; so he took hold of his father's hand to move it from Ephraim's head to Manasseh's head. [18] Joseph said to him, "No, my father, this one is the firstborn; put your right hand on his head." [19] But his father refused and said, "I know, my son, I know. He too will become a people, and he too will become great. Nevertheless, his younger brother will be greater than he, and his descendants will become a group of nations." [20] He blessed them that day and said, "In your name will Israel pronounce this blessing: 'May God make you like Ephraim and Manasseh.'" So he put Ephraim ahead of Manasseh. [21] Then Israel said to Joseph, "I am about to die, but God will be with you and take you back to the land of your fathers. [22] And to you I give one more ridge of land than to your brothers, the ridge I took from the Amorites with my sword and my bow."

*Genesis 48:15-22*

*Jehovah, thank You for the blessings, territory, and the vision of the territory.*

# APRIL 3

[15] When Joseph's brothers saw that their father was dead, they said, "What if Joseph holds a grudge against us and pays us back for all the wrongs we did to him?" [16] So they sent word to Joseph, saying, "Your father left these instructions before he died: [17] 'This is what you are to say to Joseph: I ask you to forgive your brothers the sins and the wrongs they committed in treating you so badly.' Now please forgive the sins of the servants of the God of your father." When their message came to him, Joseph wept. [18] His brothers then came and threw themselves down before him. "We are your slaves," they said. [19] But Joseph said to them, "Don't be afraid. Am I in the place of God?

*Genesis 50:15-19*

*Lord, thank You for giving my soul such peace that I do not hold a grudge, yet I love and forgive.*

# APRIL 4

[20] You intended to harm me, but God intended it for good to accomplish what is now being done, the saving of many lives. [21] So then, don't be afraid. I will provide for you and your children." And he reassured them and spoke kindly to them.

*Genesis 50:20-21*

*Lord, thank You for revelation and reason to celebrate the actual path I have traveled.*

# APRIL 5

[22] Joseph stayed in Egypt, along with all his father's family. He lived a hundred and ten years [23] and saw the third generation of Ephraim's children. Also the children of Makir son of Manasseh were placed at birth on Joseph's knees.
[24] Then Joseph said to his brothers, "I am about to die. But God will surely come to your aid and take you up out of this land to the land he promised on oath to Abraham, Isaac and Jacob." [25] And Joseph made the Israelites swear an oath and said, "God will surely come to your aid, and then you must carry my bones up from this place."
[26] So Joseph died at the age of a hundred and ten. And after they embalmed him, he was placed in a coffin in Egypt.

*Genesis 50:22-26*

*Lord, thank You for investing in me for all that You have assigned me to do. May I carry out Your will and please You.*

# APRIL 6

[5] Love the LORD Your God with all your heart and with all your soul and with all your strength.

***Deuteronomy 6:5***

*Lord, I want to love You. Help me when I don't love You and just don't want to love You.*

# APRIL 7

⁶ These commandments that I give you today are to be on your hearts.

*Deuteronomy 6:6*

_____
_____
_____
_____
_____
_____
_____
_____
_____
_____
_____
_____
_____
_____
_____
_____
_____
_____
_____
_____
_____
_____
_____
_____
_____
_____
_____
_____

*Lord, thank You for my heart and all that You give me to put on it.*

# APRIL 8

[13] Fear the Lord your God, serve him only and take your oaths in his name.

*Deuteronomy 6:13*

___

*Lord, help me to only trust You with respect, only serve You, and take oaths in Your name.*

# APRIL 9

[18] Do what is right and good in the LORD's sight, so that it may go well with you and you may go in and take over the good land the LORD promised on oath to your ancestors, [19] thrusting out all your enemies before you, as the LORD said.

*Deuteronomy 6:18-19*

*Father, help me do what is right. At all times. To show others that You are God and You are amazing.*

# APRIL 10

[7] "Be strong and very courageous. Be careful to obey all the law my servant Moses gave you; do not turn from it to the right or to the left, that you may be successful wherever you go.

*Joshua 1:7*

___

*Thank You, Father, for allowing me to be courageous in pursuit of Your will.*

# APRIL 11

⁹ Have I not commanded you? Be strong and courageous. Do not be afraid; do not be discouraged, for the LORD your God will be with you wherever you go."

*Joshua 1:9*

_____
_____
_____
_____
_____
_____
_____
_____
_____
_____
_____
_____
_____
_____
_____
_____
_____
_____
_____
_____
_____
_____
_____
_____
_____
_____
_____
_____
_____
_____

*Thank You, Master for staying with me during these transitions.*

# APRIL 12

[21] He said to the Israelites, "In the future when your descendants ask their parents, 'What do these stones mean?' [22] tell them, 'Israel crossed the Jordan on dry ground.' [23] For the LORD your God dried up the Jordan before you until you had crossed over. The LORD your God did to the Jordan what he had done to the Red Sea when he dried it up before us until we had crossed over. [24] He did this so that all the peoples of the earth might know that the hand of the LORD is powerful and so that you might always fear the LORD your God."

*Joshua 4:21-24*

*Thank You for Your provision for escape and safety, Dear Lord.*

# APRIL 13

[16] But Ruth replied, "Don't urge me to leave you or to turn back from you. Where you go I will go, and where you stay I will stay. Your people will be my people and your God my God. [17] Where you die I will die, and there I will be buried. May the LORD deal with me, be it ever so severely, if even death separates you and me."

*Ruth 1:16-17*

*Thank You, Father, for our family and our loyalty toward one another.*

# APRIL 14

[10] The LORD came and stood there, calling as at the other times, "Samuel! Samuel!" Then Samuel said, "Speak, for Your servant is listening."

*1 Samuel 3:10*

_____
_____
_____
_____
_____
_____
_____
_____
_____
_____
_____
_____
_____
_____
_____
_____
_____
_____
_____
_____
_____
_____
_____
_____
_____
_____
_____

*Lord, thank You for calling me. Thank You for being able to answer to You.*

# APRIL 15

[7] But the LORD said to Samuel, "Do not consider his appearance or his height, for I have rejected him. The LORD does not look at the things people look at. People look at the outward appearance, but the LORD looks at the heart."

*1 Samuel 16:7*

---

**Lord, remind me that You are concerned with the inside rather than the inside.**

# APRIL 16

<sup>12</sup> So he sent for him and had him brought in. He was glowing with health and had a fine appearance and handsome features. Then the LORD said, "Rise and anoint him; this is the one."

*1 Samuel 16:12*

**Lord, thank You that my handsome appearance does not stop me from serving You wholeheartedly.**

# APRIL 17

³² David said to Saul, "Let no one lose heart on account of this Philistine; your servant will go and fight him." ³³ Saul replied, "You are not able to go out against this Philistine and fight him; you are only a young man, and he has been a warrior from his youth."

*1 Samuel 17:32-33*

*Lord, thank You for showing up when others doubt and discourage me.*

# APRIL 18

[34] But David said to Saul, "Your servant has been keeping his father's sheep. When a lion or a bear came and carried off a sheep from the flock, [35] I went after it, struck it and rescued the sheep from its mouth. When it turned on me, I seized it by its hair, struck it and killed it. [36] Your servant has killed both the lion and the bear; this uncircumcised Philistine will be like one of them, because he has defied the armies of the living God. [37] The LORD who rescued me from the paw of the lion and the paw of the bear will rescue me from the hand of this Philistine." Saul said to David, "Go, and the LORD be with you."

*1 Samuel 17:34-37*

*Lord, thank You for my testimony of what You saved me from and where You have delivered me to.*

# APRIL 19

[38] Then Saul dressed David in his own tunic. He put a coat of armor on him and a bronze helmet on his head. [39] David fastened on his sword over the tunic and tried walking around, because he was not used to them. "I cannot go in these," he said to Saul, "because I am not used to them." So he took them off.

*1 Samuel 17:38-39*

*Lord, remind me and show others that I am prepared for all that You have planned for me.*

# APRIL 20

[40] Then he took his staff in his hand, chose five smooth stones from the stream, put them in the pouch of his shepherd's bag and, with his sling in his hand, approached the Philistine. [41] Meanwhile, the Philistine, with his shield bearer in front of him, kept coming closer to David. [42] He looked David over and saw that he was little more than a boy, glowing with health and handsome, and he despised him.

*1 Samuel 17:40-42*

*Master, thank You for Your provision for my battles, mentally and physically.*

# APRIL 21

[45] David said to the Philistine, "You come against me with sword and spear and javelin, but I come against you in the name of the LORD Almighty, the God of the armies of Israel, whom you have defied. [46] This day the LORD will deliver you into my hands, and I'll strike you down and cut off your head. This very day I will give the carcasses of the Philistine army to the birds and the wild animals, and the whole world will know that there is a God in Israel. [47] All those gathered here will know that it is not by sword or spear that the LORD saves; for the battle is the LORD's, and he will give all of you into our hands."

*1 Samuel 17:45-47*

*Lord, I trust You and I declare You the victor in all of my battles.*

# APRIL 22

[2] "I am about to go the way of all the earth," he said. "So be strong, act like a man, [3] and observe what the LORD your God requires: Walk in obedience to him, and keep his decrees and commands, his laws and regulations, as written in the Law of Moses. Do this so that you may prosper in all you do and wherever you go [4] and that the LORD may keep his promise to me: 'If your descendants watch how they live, and if they walk faithfully before me with all their heart and soul, you will never fail to have a successor on the throne of Israel.'

*1 Kings 2:2-4*

**Lord, thank You for the prayers and wisdom of others.**

# APRIL 23

³ Solomon showed his love for the LORD by walking according to the instructions given him by his father David, except that he offered sacrifices and burned incense on the high places.

*1 Kings 3:3*

**Lord, thank You for an example of obedience and service which pleases You.**

# APRIL 24

⁶ Solomon answered, "You have shown great kindness to your servant, my father David, because he was faithful to you and righteous and upright in heart. You have continued this great kindness to him and have given him a son to sit on his throne this very day.
⁷ "Now, LORD my God, you have made your servant king in place of my father David. But I am only a little child and do not know how to carry out my duties. ⁸ Your servant is here among the people you have chosen, a great people, too numerous to count or number. ⁹ So give your servant a discerning heart to govern your people and to distinguish between right and wrong. For who is able to govern this great people of yours?"

*1 Kings 3:6-9*

*Lord, thank You for hearing me when I pray; I pray to discern and have wisdom and to serve You.*

# APRIL 25

[10] The Lord was pleased that Solomon had asked for this. [11] So God said to him, "Since you have asked for this and not for long life or wealth for yourself, nor have asked for the death of your enemies but for discernment in administering justice, [12] I will do what you have asked. I will give you a wise and discerning heart, so that there will never have been anyone like you, nor will there ever be. [13] Moreover, I will give you what you have not asked for—both wealth and honor—so that in your lifetime you will have no equal among kings. [14] And if you walk in obedience to me and keep my decrees and commands as David your father did, I will give you a long life."

*1 Kings 3:10-14*

*Lord, thank You for hearing, answering my prayers, and giving me more than I asked for.*

# APRIL 26

[8] Then the LORD said to Satan, "Have you considered my servant Job? There is no one on earth like him; he is blameless and upright, a man who fears God and shuns evil."

*Job 1:8*

*Thank You, Master for a great report about me; I am proud to make You happy.*

# APRIL 27

⁹"Does Job fear God for nothing?" Satan replied. ¹⁰"Have you not put a hedge around him and his household and everything he has? You have blessed the work of his hands, so that his flocks and herds are spread throughout the land. ¹¹ But now stretch out your hand and strike everything he has, and he will surely curse you to your face."

*Job 1:9-11*

*Lord, thank You for letting others see how well You bless me.*

# APRIL 28

[12] The LORD said to Satan, "Very well, then, everything he has is in your power, but on the man himself do not lay a finger." Then Satan went out from the presence of the LORD.

*Job 1:12*

*Master, thank You for your protection from the very hand of satan.*

# APRIL 29

[20] At this, Job got up and tore his robe and shaved his head. Then he fell to the ground in worship [21] and said:

"Naked I came from my mother's womb,
  and naked I will depart.
The LORD gave and the LORD has taken away;
  may the name of the LORD be praised."

*Job 1:20-21*

---

*Lord, I realize that everything I have, You gave it to me; I hope that I am the steward You designated me to be.*

# APRIL 30

[22] In all this, Job did not sin by charging God with wrongdoing.

*Job 1:22*

*Lord, please help me not to sin . . . EVER.*

# YOUR PERSONAL TESTIMONY

Why do you need a personal testimony? Better question, why do you need to share your testimony? Your testimony was designed to share with others. This personal encounter with God is designed to elevate them and their spirit to a new level where more growth and development can occur. Don't be surprised when you experience some growth and development, too.

When did you accept Jesus into your heart? When have you recognized God for being in your life and moving you to the right place? When had God done the opposite of what you asked but it was better than you expected? When has God simply provided you His peace?

Spend about 15 minutes writing the answers to these questions, while considering how you would share these answers and with whom you would share the answers.

_____
_____
_____
_____
_____
_____
_____
_____
_____
_____
_____
_____
_____
_____
_____
_____
_____
_____
_____
_____
_____
_____

# MAY 1

³ Then the LORD said to Satan, "Have you considered my servant Job? There is no one on earth like him; he is blameless and upright, a man who fears God and shuns evil. And he still maintains his integrity, though you incited me against him to ruin him without any reason."
⁴ "Skin for skin!" Satan replied. "A man will give all he has for his own life. ⁵ But now stretch out your hand and strike his flesh and bones, and he will surely curse you to your face."
⁶ The LORD said to Satan, "Very well, then, he is in your hands; but you must spare his life."
⁷ So Satan went out from the presence of the LORD and afflicted Job with painful sores from the soles of his feet to the crown of his head. ⁸ Then Job took a piece of broken pottery and scraped himself with it as he sat among the ashes.
⁹ His wife said to him, "Are you still maintaining your integrity? Curse God and die!"
¹⁰ He replied, "You are talking like a foolish woman. Shall we accept good from God, and not trouble?"
In all this, Job did not sin in what he said.

*Job 2:3-10*

*Master, thank You for the example Job is—his wisdom, his focus, and his perseverance.*

# MAY 2

[8] "But if I were you, I would appeal to God;
I would lay my cause before Him.

*Job 5:8*

*Father, thank You for reminding me of Your power.*

# MAY 3

⁸ "Oh, that I might have my request,
   that God would grant what I hope for,
⁹ that God would be willing to crush me,
   to let loose his hand and cut off my life!
¹⁰ Then I would still have this consolation—
   my joy in unrelenting pain—
   that I had not denied the words of the Holy One.

*Job 6:8-10*

_____
_____
_____
_____
_____
_____
_____
_____
_____
_____
_____
_____
_____
_____
_____
_____
_____
_____
_____
_____
_____
_____
_____
_____
_____
_____

*Lord, thank You for reminding me of how much I depend on You.*

# MAY 4

⁵ But if you will seek God earnestly
  and plead with the Almighty,
⁶ if you are pure and upright,
  even now he will rouse himself on your behalf
  and restore you to your prosperous state.

*Job 8:5-6*

*Lord, thank You for Your fairness and keeping cover over me.*

# MAY 5

$^{23}$ The Almighty is beyond our reach and exalted in power;
   in His justice and great righteousness, He does not oppress.
$^{24}$ Therefore, people revere Him,
   for does He not have regard for all the wise in heart?"

*Job 37:23-24*

*Daddy, thank You for the great things that You do which are beyond my understanding.*

# MAY 6

[4] "Where were you when I laid the earth's foundation?
   Tell me, if you understand.
[5] Who marked off its dimensions? Surely you know!
   Who stretched a measuring line across it?

*Job 38:4-5*

*Lord, thank You for listening to me, especially when I am out of line.*

# MAY 7

[26] "Does the hawk take flight by your wisdom and spread its wings toward the south?
[27] Does the eagle soar at your command and build its nest on high?

*Job 39:26-27*

*Lrod, thank You for pointing out how we are extremely different and that I have no clue.*

# MAY 8

³ Then Job answered the LORD:
⁴ "I am unworthy—how can I reply to You? I put my hand over my mouth.
⁵ I spoke once, but I have no answer—twice, but I will say no more."

*Job 40:3-5*

**Thank You, Father, for the miraculous things You do!**

# MAY 9

[10] No one is fierce enough to rouse it. Who then is able to stand against Me?

*Job 41:10*

***Lord, I am amazed at ALL that You do.***

# MAY 10

Then Job replied to the LORD:
² "I know that You can do all things; no purpose of Yours can be thwarted.
³ You asked, 'Who is this that obscures My plans without knowledge?'
   Surely I spoke of things I did not understand, things too wonderful for me to know.
⁴ "You said, 'Listen now, and I will speak; I will question you, and you shall answer me.'
⁵ My ears had heard of You but now my eyes have seen You.
⁶ Therefore I despise myself and repent in dust and ashes."

*Job 42:1-6*

*Thank You for reminding me that I do not understand You and what You do.*

# MAY 11

⁷ After the LORD had said these things to Job, he said to Eliphaz the Temanite, "I am angry with you and your two friends, because you have not spoken the truth about me, as my servant Job has. ⁸ So now take seven bulls and seven rams and go to my servant Job and sacrifice a burnt offering for yourselves. My servant Job will pray for you, and I will accept his prayer and not deal with you according to your folly. You have not spoken the truth about me, as my servant Job has." ⁹ So Eliphaz the Temanite, Bildad the Shuhite and Zophar the Naamathite did what the LORD told them; and the LORD accepted Job's prayer.

¹⁰ After Job had prayed for his friends, the LORD restored his fortunes and gave him twice as much as he had before. ¹¹ All his brothers and sisters and everyone who had known him before came and ate with him in his house. They comforted and consoled him over all the trouble the LORD had brought on him, and each one gave him a piece of silver and a gold ring.

¹² The LORD blessed the latter part of Job's life more than the former part. He had fourteen thousand sheep, six thousand camels, a thousand yoke of oxen and a thousand donkeys. ¹³ And he also had seven sons and three daughters. ¹⁴ The first daughter he named Jemimah, the second Keziah and the third Keren-Happuch. ¹⁵ Nowhere in all the land were there found women as beautiful as Job's daughters, and their father granted them an inheritance along with their brothers.

¹⁶ After this, Job lived a hundred and forty years; he saw his children and their children to the fourth generation. ¹⁷ And so Job died, an old man and full of years.

*Job 42:7-17*

*Lord, thank You for restoration and blessings.*

# MAY 12

[1] Blessed is the one who does not walk in step with the wicked or stand in the way that sinners take or sit in the company of mockers, [2] but whose delight is in the law of the LORD, and who meditates on His law day and night.

*Psalm 1:1-2*

*Help me, Father to meditate on Your word purposefully.*

## MAY 13

[11] Serve the LORD with fear and celebrate His rule with trembling.
[12] Kiss His son, or He will be angry and your way will lead to your destruction, for His wrath can flare up in a moment. Blessed are all who take refuge in Him.

*Psalm 2:11-12*

_____

*Thank You, for claiming me as Your own child, Lord.*

# MAY 14

³ But You, LORD, are a shield around me, my glory, the One who lifts my head high.
⁴ I call out to the LORD, and He answers me from His holy mountain.

*Psalm 3:3-4*

**Lord, thank You for being my shield.**

# MAY 15

[1] Answer me when I call to you, my righteous God. Give me relief from my distress; have mercy on me and hear my prayer.

*Psalm 4:1*

*Lord, I am in need of Your relief in my times of distress.*

# MAY 16

[11] But let all who take refuge in You be glad; let them ever sing for joy. Spread Your protection over them, that those who love Your name may rejoice in You.
[12] Surely, LORD, You bless the righteous; You surround them with Your favor as with a shield..
*Psalm 5:11-12*

**Lord, thank You for hearing my cry and plea.**

# MAY 17

¹ LORD, do not rebuke me in Your anger or discipline me in Your wrath.
² Have mercy on me, LORD, for I am faint; heal me, LORD, for my bones are in agony.
³ My soul is in deep anguish. How long, LORD, how long?
⁴ Turn, LORD, and deliver me; save me because of Your unfailing love.

*Psalm 6:1-4*

_____
_____
_____
_____
_____
_____
_____
_____
_____
_____
_____
_____
_____
_____
_____
_____
_____
_____
_____
_____
_____
_____
_____
_____
_____
_____
_____
_____
_____

**Lord, I am in anguish and pray for Your relief from Your discipline and wrath.**

# MAY 18

[10] My shield is God Most High, who saves the upright in heart.
[11] God is a righteous judge, a God who displays his wrath every day.

*Psalm 7:10-11*

*Master, thank You for recognizing my righteousness.*

# MAY 19

[1] O LORD, Our Lord, how excellent is thy name in all the earth! who hast set thy glory above the heavens.

*Psalm 8:1 KJV*

*Lord, how majestic is Your name in all the Earth.*

# MAY 20

[1] I will give thanks to You, LORD, with all my heart;
  I will tell of all Your wonderful deeds.
[2] I will be glad and rejoice in You;
  I will sing the praises of Your name, O Most High.

*Psalm 9:1-2*

*Lord, thank You with all of my heart, and help me to continue to share with others Your greatness and wonderful deeds.*

# MAY 21

[1] Why, LORD, do You stand far off?
  Why do You hide Yourself in times of trouble?

*Psalm 10:1*

---

*Lord, please don't distance Yourself from me.*

# MAY 22

[4] The LORD is in His holy temple; the LORD is on His heavenly throne. He observes everyone on earth; His eyes examine them.
[5] The LORD examines the righteous, but the wicked, those who love violence, He hates with a passion.

*Psalm 11:4-5*

*Lord, thank You for being my refuge.*

# MAY 23

[1] Help, LORD, for no one is faithful anymore; those who are loyal have vanished from the human race.
[2] Everyone lies to their neighbor; they flatter with their lips but harbor deception in their hearts.

*Psalm 12:1-2*

*Father, thank You for protecting me from the wicked.*

# MAY 24

¹ How long, LORD? Will You forget me forever?
  How long will You hide Your face from me?
² How long must I wrestle with my thoughts
  and day after day have sorrow in my heart?
  How long will my enemy triumph over me?

*Psalm 13:1-2*

_____
_____
_____
_____
_____
_____
_____
_____
_____
_____
_____
_____
_____
_____
_____
_____
_____
_____
_____
_____
_____
_____
_____
_____

*Master, please do not hide Your face from me.*

# MAY 25

² The LORD looks down from heaven on all mankind to see if there are any who understand, any who seek God.
³ All have turned away, all have become corrupt; there is no one who does good, not even one.

*Psalm 14:2-3*

*I am not good. Please help me to be righteous.*

# MAY 26

[1] LORD, who may dwell in Your sacred tent? Who may live on Your holy mountain?
[2] The one whose walk is blameless, who does what is righteous, who speaks the truth from their heart;
[3] whose tongue utters no slander, who does no wrong to a neighbor, and casts no slur on others;
[4] who despises a vile person but honors those who fear the LORD; who keeps an oath even when it hurts, and does not change their mind;
[5] who lends money to the poor without interest; who does not accept a bribe against the innocent. Whoever does these things will never be shaken.

*Psalm 15*

*I want so badly to live a life unshaken. Lord, please help me.*

# MAY 27

[1] Keep me safe, my God, for in You I take refuge.
[2] I say to the LORD, "You are my Lord; apart from You I have no good thing."

*Psalm 16:1-2*

*Lord, apart from You I am nothing and have no good thing.*

# MAY 28

[3] Though You probe my heart, though You examine me at night and test me, You will find that I have planned no evil; my mouth has not transgressed.
[4] Though people tried to bribe me, I have kept myself from the ways of the violent through what Your lips have commanded.

*Psalm 17:3-4*

*Jehovah, thank You for keeping me on Your path and not letting my feet stumble.*

# MAY 29

¹ I love You, LORD, my strength.
² The LORD is my rock, my fortress and my deliverer;
my God is my rock, in whom I take refuge,
my shield and the horn of my salvation, my stronghold.

*Psalm 18:1-2*

___

**Lord, You are my strength, my fortress, my deliverer, my rock, my refuge, my work of my salvation and my stronghold.**

# MAY 30

[14] May these words of my mouth and this meditation of my heart be pleasing in Your sight, LORD, my Rock and my Redeemer.

*Psalm 19:14*

*Lord, may the words of my mouth and the meditation of my heart please You.*

# MAY 31

[1] May the LORD answer you when you are in distress; may the name of the God of Jacob protect you.

*Psalm 20:1*

*Father, thank You for answering me in my distress.*

# JUNE 1

⁷ For the king trusts in the LORD; through the unfailing love of the Most High. He will not be shaken.

*Psalm 21:7*

*Lord, I rejoice in Your strength!*

# JUNE 2

[1] My God, my God, why have You forsaken me?
 Why are You so far from saving me, so far from my cries of anguish?
[2] My God, I cry out by day, but You do not answer, by night, but I find no rest.

*Psalm 22:1-2*

**Father, please be attentive to my cries of anguish.**

# JUNE 3

[1] The LORD is my shepherd, I lack nothing.
[2] He makes me lie down in green pastures, He leads me beside quiet waters,
[3] He refreshes my soul. He guides me along the right paths for His name's sake.
[4] Even though I walk through the darkest valley, I will fear no evil, for You are with me; Your rod and Your staff, they comfort me.
[5] You prepare a table before me in the presence of my enemies. You anoint my head with oil; my cup overflows.
[6] Surely Your goodness and love will follow me all the days of my life, and I will dwell in the house of the LORD forever.

*Psalm 23*

*Thank You for leading me beside the still water and restoring my soul, Lord.*

# JUNE 4

[1] The earth is the LORD's, and everything in it, the world, and all who live in it;
[2] for He founded it on the seas and established it on the waters.

*Psalm 24:1-2*

*Lord, thank You for claiming me as Your own.*

# JUNE 5

[1] In You, LORD my God, I put my trust.
[4] Show me Your ways, LORD, teach me Your paths.

*Psalm 25:1, 4*

*Lord, I trust You. Help me when I don't.*

# JUNE 6

[2] Test me, LORD, and try me, examine my heart and my mind;
[3] for I have always been mindful of Your unfailing love and have lived in reliance on Your faithfulness.

*Psalm 26:2-3*

*Test me, Lord, and try me, examine my heart and my mind.*

# JUNE 7

[1] The LORD is my light and my salvation—
whom shall I fear?
The LORD is the stronghold of my life—
of whom shall I be afraid?

*Psalm 27:1*

*You, Lord, are my light and my salvation, whom shall I fear.*

# JUNE 8

⁸ The LORD is the strength of His people, a fortress of salvation for His anointed one.
⁹ Save Your people and bless Your inheritance; be their shepherd and carry them forever.

*Psalm 28:8-9*

*Lord, remind me not to repay evil deeds or harbor malice in my heart.*

# JUNE 9

[3] The voice of the LORD is over the waters; the God of glory thunders, the LORD thunders over the mighty waters.
[4] The voice of the LORD is powerful; the voice of the LORD is majestic.

*Psalm 29:3-4*

*Thank You, Lord, for Your majestic and powerful voice; Your holiness and splendor.*

# JUNE 10

[1] I will exalt You, LORD, for You lifted me out of the depths and did not let my enemies gloat over me.
[2] LORD My God, I called to You for help, and You healed me.
[3] You, LORD, brought me up from the realm of the dead; you spared me from going down to the pit.

*Psalm 30:1-3*

*Thank You for exalting me and lifting me out the depths of what hurts me.*

# JUNE 11

[1] In You, LORD, I have taken refuge; let me never be put to shame; deliver me in Your righteousness.
[2] Turn Your ear to me, come quickly to my rescue; be my rock of refuge, a strong fortress to save me.
[3] Since You are my rock and my fortress, for the sake of Your name lead and guide me.
[4] Keep me free from the trap that is set for me, for You are my refuge.
[5] Into Your hands I commit my spirit; deliver me, LORD, my faithful God.

*Psalm 31:1-5*

*Lord, help me never put You to shame based on my behavior, heart and attitude.*

# JUNE 12

[1] Blessed is the one whose transgressions are forgiven, whose sins are covered.
[2] Blessed is the one whose sin the LORD does not count against them and in whose spirit is no deceit.

*Psalm 32:1-2*

---

*Thank You, Master, for forgiving my transgressions and covering my sins.*

# JUNE 13

[20] We wait in hope for the LORD; He is our help and our shield.
[21] In Him our hearts rejoice, for we trust in His holy name.
[22] May Your unfailing love be with us, LORD, even as we put our hope in You.

*Psalm 33:20-22*

*Lord, thank You for Your plans and canceling the plans and for covering my sins.*

# JUNE 14

¹ I will extol the LORD at all times; His praise will always be on my lips.
² I will glory in the LORD; let the afflicted hear and rejoice.
³ Glorify the LORD with me; let us exalt His name together.

*Psalm 34:1-3*

_____

**Lord, I will bless the You at all times; praise will always be on my lips.**

# JUNE 15

¹ Contend, LORD, with those who contend with me; fight against those who fight against me.
² Take up shield and armor; arise and come to my aid.
³ Brandish spear and javelin against those who pursue me.
Say to me, "I am your salvation."

*Psalm 35:1-3*

*Lord, please fight my battles and my enemies.*

# JUNE 16

[2] In their own eyes they flatter themselves too much to detect or hate their sin.
[3] The words of their mouths are wicked and deceitful; they fail to act wisely or do good.

*Psalm 36:2-3*

*Lord, You are love and You are salvation.*

# JUNE 17

³ Trust in the LORD and do good; dwell in the land and enjoy safe pasture.
⁴ Take delight in the LORD, and He will give you the desires of your heart.

*Psalm 37:3-4*

*I will delight in You Lord and I pray that You give me the desires of my heart, according to Your will.*

# JUNE 18

¹ LORD, do not rebuke me in Your anger or discipline me in Your wrath.
² Your arrows have pierced me, and Your hand has come down on me.
³ Because of your wrath there is no health in my body; there is no soundness in my bones because of my sin.
⁴ My guilt has overwhelmed me like a burden too heavy to bear.

*Psalm 38:1-4*

**Lord, I do not want to be subject to Your anger or Your wrath.**

# JUNE 19

[1] I said, "I will watch my ways and keep my tongue from sin; I will put a muzzle on my mouth while in the presence of the wicked."
[2] So I remained utterly silent, not even saying anything good. But my anguish increased;
[3] my heart grew hot within me.

*Psalm 39:1-3*

**Lord, I will keep my tongue from sin and keep careful watch over my mouth; will Your guidance.**

# JUNE 20

¹ I waited patiently for the LORD; He turned to me and heard my cry.
⁴ Blessed is the one who trusts in the LORD, who does not look to the proud, to those who turn aside to false gods.
⁵ Many, LORD my God, are the wonders You have done, the things You planned for us. None can compare with You; were I to speak and tell of Your deeds, they would be too many to declare.

*Psalm 40:1, 4-5*

*Lord, help me to remain patient while I wait on You to carry out Your will.*

# JUNE 21

[1] Blessed are those who have regard for the weak; the LORD delivers them in times of trouble.
[2] The LORD protects and preserves them—they are counted among the blessed in the land—
He does not give them over to the desire of their foes.
[3] The LORD sustains them on their sickbed and restores them from their bed of illness.

*Psalm 41:1-3*

*Lord, help me remember those with less confidence and fewer talents with favor and treat them with love.*

# JUNE 22

[1] As the deer pants for streams of water, so my soul pants for You, my God.
[2] My soul thirsts for God, for the living God. When can I go and meet with God?

*Psalm 42:1-2*

*God, my soul pants for You. I am waiting to meet You.*

# JUNE 23

⁵ Why, my soul, are you downcast? Why so disturbed within me?
Put your hope in God, for I will yet praise Him, my Savior and my God.

*Psalm 43:5*

*Thank You for being my strong tower, God.*

# JUNE 24

[1] We have heard it with our ears, O God; our ancestors have told us what You did in their days, in days long ago.
[2] With Your hand You drove out the nations and planted our ancestors; You crushed the peoples and made our ancestors flourish.

*Psalm 44:1-2*

___

*God, thank You for those who share what You have done for them.*

# JUNE 25

[17] I will perpetuate Your memory through all generations; therefore the nations will praise You for ever and ever.

*Psalm 45:17*

*Lord, thank You for times of celebration.*

# JUNE 26

[1] God is our refuge and strength, an ever-present help in trouble.
[10] He says, "Be still, and know that I am God;
   I will be exalted among the nations,
   I will be exalted in the earth."

*Psalm 46:1, 10*

*Lord, help me to recognize when I need to be still.*

# JUNE 27

² For the LORD Most High is awesome, the great King over all the earth.
³ He subdued nations under us, peoples under our feet.

*Psalm 47:2-3*

**Thank You God for what You do for us.**

# JUNE 28

[1] Great is the LORD, and most worthy of praise, in the city of our God, His holy mountain.
*Psalm 48:1*

*Lord, remind me to meditate on Your unfailing love.*

# JUNE 29

[3] My mouth will speak words of wisdom; the meditation of my heart will give you understanding.

*Psalm 49:3*

*Master, thank You for the wisdom that I need to share with others.*

# JUNE 30

[7] "Listen, My people, and I will speak; I will testify against you, Israel: I am God, your God.
*Psalm 50:7*

*Lord, thank You for choosing me and being my God.*

# DEVELOPING YOUR PRAYER LIFE— PART TWO

A component of prayer and a developing prayer life is intercessory prayer. This type of prayer is when you pray for others. Why don't they pray for themselves? Like yourself, they may not be able to pray for themselves or they don't know to pray or they may need some extra support.

A common intercessory prayer is one of salvation for someone who is not saved. But this type of prayer could include everything. When I am not about to see clearly my path or when huge decisions face me, I solicit the prayers of my prayer warriors and they pray for me. They may ask God for cover and protection. They may ask God for my increased wisdom about the issue. They may ask god to offer me His peace during whatever storm may be around.

Whatever they pray, they go to God in my place. In this instance, I am also still praying but I needed some help.

But when I need to be the intercessor? I prayed for my mother before I knew the definition, as did my grandmother. We were praying for the same reasons but at different levels. At six years old, my prayer probably followed this format:

> "God, Mommy cries a lot and can't smile at me. She doesn't say much when we drive home. She has a lot of marks on her body and when I ask, she gets really nervous. I saw Daddy hit her with a belt. Please make him stop. Amen."

When I was eight, they divorced, I was really sad initially because she still wasn't talking to me. I thought I had done something.

At age twelve, the prayer was 'thank You Lord for bringing my mother to church. I really like it that we go to church together.'

At 27, my prayer was 'thank You Lord for bringing Papa into her life and all that they experienced together. Now that he's with You, offer her comfort and peace and means for the rest of her journey.'

Intercession is bridging the gap between us and God. Intercession does not require the other's permission, nor do you have to tell them you prayed for them.

God sent the Holy Spirit, the third portion of the Trinity, to intercede for us. He petitions to God for us in many situations. The Holy Spirit has an assignment. Romans 8:26 reads, "In the same way, the Spirit helps us in our weakness. We do not know what we ought to pray for, but the Spirit Himself intercedes for us with groans that words cannot express." So when you don't know what to pray for, then know that the Holy Spirit is there interceding for you and each of your needs.

One last point about developing your prayer life. You will always mature in your walk and your prayer life will increase. Also, remember that prayer is daily and without ceasing. Try to avoid praying only when there is crisis. While God is all-powerful and performs crisis intervention daily, He does not prefer this method.

Your intimacy with God will reshape and mold and shape you to be more like Christ, the way He designed us—in His own image.

MINISTER GAGE

# JULY 1

[10] Create in me a pure heart, O God,
 and renew a steadfast spirit within me.
[11] Do not cast me from your presence
 or take your Holy Spirit from me.
[12] Restore to me the joy of your salvation
 and grant me a willing spirit, to sustain me.

*Psalm 51:10-12*

_____
_____
_____
_____
_____
_____
_____
_____
_____
_____
_____
_____
_____
_____
_____
_____
_____
_____
_____
_____
_____
_____
_____
_____

*Thank You for having mercy on me, giving me Your unfailing love, and blotting out my transgressions.*

# JULY 2

⁸ But I am like an olive tree flourishing in the house of God;
I trust in God's unfailing love for ever and ever.
⁹ For what You have done I will always praise You in the presence of Your faithful people.
And I will hope in Your name, for Your name is good.

*Psalm 52:8-9*

_____
_____
_____
_____
_____
_____
_____
_____
_____
_____
_____
_____
_____
_____
_____
_____
_____
_____
_____
_____
_____
_____
_____
_____
_____
_____
_____

*Lord, help me to resist evil and avoid sin, so that I can avoid Your wrath.*

# JULY 3

[1] The fool says in his heart, "There is no God."
They are corrupt, and their ways are vile; there is no one who does good.

*Psalm 53:1*

*Lord, let me be wise rather than foolish.*

# JULY 4

[3] Arrogant foes are attacking me; ruthless people are trying to kill me—people without regard for God.
[4] Surely God is my help; the Lord is the one who sustains me.

*Psalm 54:3-4*

*Thank You Lord, for delivering me from my troubles.*

# JULY 5

[4] My heart is in anguish within me; the terrors of death have fallen on me.
[5] Fear and trembling have beset me; horror has overwhelmed me.

*Psalm 55:4-5*

*Lord, my heart is in anguish and I need Your relief; help me please.*

# JULY 6

[1] Be merciful to me, my God, for my enemies are in hot pursuit; all day long they press their attack.
[2] My adversaries pursue me all day long; in their pride many are attacking me.
[3] When I am afraid, I put my trust in You.

*Psalm 56:1-3*

___

*Father, give me energy for the enemies which chase me, so that I don't quit or make a mistake.*

# JULY 7

[7] My heart, O God, is steadfast, my heart is steadfast; I will sing and make music.
[8] Awake, my soul! Awake, harp and lyre! I will awaken the dawn.

*Psalm 57:7-8*

*God, thank You for a steadfast heart—one that I can please You with.*

# JULY 8

[10] The righteous will be glad when they are avenged, when they dip their feet in the blood of the wicked.
[11] Then people will say, "Surely the righteous still are rewarded; surely there is a God who judges the earth."

*Psalm 58:10-11*

---

*Whether You reward the righteous or not, as I would like, Your favor is good enough, Lord.*

# JULY 9

[16] But I will sing of your strength, in the morning I will sing of Your love for You are my fortress, my refuge in times of trouble.
[17] You are my strength, I sing praise to You; You, God, are my fortress, my God on whom I can rely.

*Psalm 59:16-17*

_____
_____
_____
_____
_____
_____
_____
_____
_____
_____
_____
_____
_____
_____
_____
_____
_____
_____
_____
_____
_____
_____
_____
_____
_____
_____
_____
_____
_____

*God, You are my strength and my fortress, on whom I can rely.*

# JULY 10

[11] Give us aid against the enemy, for human help is worthless.
[12] With God we will gain the victory, and He will trample down our enemies.

*Psalm 60:11-12*

*God, I beg You to release me from Your angry and restore me.*

# JULY 11

¹ Hear my cry, O God; listen to my prayer.
² From the ends of the earth I call to You, I call as my heart grows faint; lead me to the rock that is higher than I.
³ For You have been my refuge, a strong tower against the foe.

*Psalm 61:1-3*

*God, I will dwell with You forever, regardless of the desire sometimes to not to.*

# JULY 12

[1] Truly my soul finds rest in God; my salvation comes from Him.
[2] Truly He is my rock and my salvation; He is my fortress, I will never be shaken.

*Psalm 62:1-2*

*My Rock and My Salvation—My God—for all that disturbs me. Lord, help my soul rest.*

# JULY 13

[1] You, God, are my God, earnestly I seek You;
I thirst for You, my whole being longs for You,
in a dry and parched land where there is no water.

*Psalm 63:1*

___

**Lord, I earnestly seek You and thirst for You.**

# JULY 14

[10] The righteous will rejoice in the LORD and take refuge in Him; all the upright in heart will glory in Him!

*Psalm 64:10*

*Forgive me for complaining, God. I have no right to complain.*

# JULY 15

[1] Praise awaits You, our God, in Zion; to You our vows will be fulfilled.
[2] You who answer prayer, to You all people will come.

*Psalm 65:1-2*

_____

*You such an awesome God. Thank You.*

# JULY 16

[1] Shout for joy to God, all the earth!
[2] Sing the glory of His name; make His praise glorious.
[3] Say to God, "How awesome are Your deeds! So great is Your power that Your enemies cringe before You.
[4] All the earth bows down to You; they sing praise to You, they sing the praises of Your name."

*Psalm 66:1-4*

*I will shout to You, God. I will praise You and glorify You.*

# JULY 17

¹ May God be gracious to us and bless us and make His face shine on us—
² so that Your ways may be known on earth, Your salvation among all nations.

*Psalm 67:1-2*

*Lord, thank You for blessing me, being gracious unto me, and making Your face to shine upon me.*

# JULY 18

[1] May God arise, may His enemies be scattered; may His foes flee before Him.
[2] May you blow them away like smoke—as wax melts before the fire, may the wicked perish before God.
[3] But may the righteous be glad and rejoice before God; may they be happy and joyful.

*Psalm 68:1-3*

*I will sing praises to You, God.*

# JULY 19

⁶ Lord, the LORD Almighty, may those who hope in You not be disgraced because of me; God of Israel, may those who seek You not be put to shame because of me.

*Psalm 69:6*

*Save me God from the high waters around my neck and save me from myself.*

# JULY 20

¹ Hasten, O God, to save me; come quickly, LORD, to help me.
⁵ But as for me, I am poor and needy; come quickly to me, O God.
You are my help and my deliverer; LORD, do not delay.

*Psalm 70:1, 5*

___

*I need You to save me from my enemies. Lord, You are great!*

# JULY 21

[15] My mouth will tell of Your righteous deeds, of Your saving acts all day long—though I know not how to relate them all.
[16] I will come and proclaim Your mighty acts, Sovereign LORD; I will proclaim Your righteous deeds, Yours alone.
[23] My lips will shout for joy when I sing praise to You—I whom You have delivered.
[24] My tongue will tell of Your righteous acts all day long, for those who wanted to harm me have been put to shame and confusion.

*Psalm 71:15-16, 23-24*

*Sovereign Lord, You are my only hope and my only refuge.*

# JULY 22

¹⁸ Praise be to the LORD God, the God of Israel, who alone does marvelous deeds.
¹⁹ Praise be to His glorious name forever; may the whole earth be filled with His glory. Amen and Amen.

*Psalm 72:18-19*

*Lord, You don't need me to tell You how marvelous You are, but You do a marvelous work.*

# JULY 23

<sup>27</sup> Those who are far from You will perish; You destroy all who are unfaithful to You.
<sup>28</sup> But as for me, it is good to be near God. I have made the Sovereign LORD my refuge; I will tell of all Your deeds.

*Psalm 73:27-28*

*Lord, forgive me for paying attention to the wrong thing and people. I will keep my focus totally on You and only You.*

# JULY 24

[21] Do not let the oppressed retreat in disgrace; may the poor and needy praise Your name.
[22] Rise up, O God, and defend Your cause; remember how fools mock You all day long.
[23] Do not ignore the clamor of Your adversaries, the uproar of Your enemies, which rises continually.

*Psalm 74:21-23*

*I apologize for angering You, Father.*

# JULY 25

[1] We praise You, God, we praise You, for Your Name is near; people tell of Your wonderful deeds.

*Psalm 75:1*

---

*I praise You God because You are God and God alone.*

# JULY 26

[7] It is You alone who are to be feared. Who can stand before You when You are angry?

*Psalm 76:7*

*Lord, I vow to serve You in every way possible with my whole heart.*

# JULY 27

[1] I cried out to God for help; I cried out to God to hear me.
[2] When I was in distress, I sought the Lord; at night I stretched out untiring hands, and I would not be comforted.
[3] I remembered You, God, and I groaned; I meditated, and my spirit grew faint.

*Psalm 77:1-3*

_____
_____
_____
_____
_____
_____
_____
_____
_____
_____
_____
_____
_____
_____
_____
_____
_____
_____
_____
_____
_____
_____
_____
_____
_____
_____
_____
_____

**Lord, I have many questions about why I have trouble and why does it last so long, but I do not question Your love.**

# JULY 28

[1] My people, hear my teaching; listen to the words of my mouth.
[2] I will open my mouth with a parable; I will utter hidden things, things from of old—
[3] things we have heard and known, things our ancestors have told us.

*Psalm 78:1-3*

*Lord, thank You for those who are designed to hold me accountable.*

# JULY 29

[13] Then we Your people, the sheep of Your pasture, will praise You forever; from generation to generation we will proclaim Your praise.

*Psalm 79:13*

*Father, thank You for letting me be Your people. Please forgive me when I act like I am not.*

# JULY 30

[19] Restore us, LORD God Almighty; make Your face shine on us, that we may be saved.
*Psalm 80:19*

*Lord, please restore me. I am so delighted, broken, and battered that it interferes with my worship, praise and service.*

# JULY 31

I heard an unknown voice say:
⁶ "I removed the burden from their shoulders; their hands were set free from the basket.
⁷ In your distress you called and I rescued you, I answered you out of a thundercloud; I tested you at the waters of Meribah.

*Psalm 81:5b-7*

*Thank You, God for hearing me and rescuing me for I know that I am unworthy.*

# AUGUST 1

[2] "How long will You defend the unjust and show partiality to the wicked?
[3] Defend the weak and the fatherless; uphold the cause of the poor and the oppressed.
[4] Rescue the weak and the needy;deliver them from the hand of the wicked.

*Psalm 82:2-4*

_____
_____
_____
_____
_____
_____
_____
_____
_____
_____
_____
_____
_____
_____
_____
_____
_____
_____
_____
_____
_____
_____
_____
_____
_____
_____
_____
_____
_____
_____

*Be compassionate when You judge me God. I need mercy that I do not deserve.*

# AUGUST 2

[17] May they ever be ashamed and dismayed; may they perish in disgrace.
[18] Let them know that You, whose name is the LORD—that You alone are the Most High over all the earth.

*Psalm 83:17-18*

_____
_____
_____
_____
_____
_____
_____
_____
_____
_____
_____
_____
_____
_____
_____
_____
_____
_____
_____
_____
_____
_____
_____
_____
_____
_____
_____
_____
_____
_____

**Lord, You alone are the Most High over all the Earth.**

# AUGUST 3

[1] How lovely is Your dwelling place, LORD Almighty!
[2] My soul yearns, even faints, for the courts of the LORD; my heart and my flesh cry out for the living God.
[3] Even the sparrow has found a home, and the swallow a nest for herself, where she may have her young—a place near Your altar, LORD Almighty, my King and my God.
[4] Blessed are those who dwell in Your house; they are ever praising You.

*Psalm 84:1-4*

*Lord Almighty, I thirst and yearn and cry for You. I cry out for You. I need You.*

# AUGUST 4

¹ You, LORD, showed favor to Your land; You restored the fortunes of Jacob.
² You forgave the iniquity of Your people and covered all their sins.
³ You set aside all Your wrath and turned from Your fierce anger
⁴ Restore us again, God our Savior, and put away Your displeasure toward us.
⁵ Will You be angry with us forever? Will You prolong Your anger through all generations?
⁶ Will You not revive us again, that Your people may rejoice in You?
⁷ Show us your unfailing love, LORD, and grant us Your salvation.

*Psalm 85:4-7*

*When You forgave me and set aside all of Your wrath and turned away Your fierce anger, God You granted me unmerited favor.*

# AUGUST 5

⁵ You, Lord, are forgiving and good, abounding in love to all who call to You.
⁶ Hear my prayer, LORD; listen to my cry for mercy.
⁷ When I am in distress, I call to You, because You answer me.

*Psalm 86:5-7*

*You, Lord, are forgiving and good, offering abounding love, which I sometimes reject. Thank You for allowing me call to You.*

# AUGUST 6

⁵ Indeed, of Zion it will be said, "This one and that one were born in her, and the Most High Himself will establish her."
⁶ The LORD will write in the register of the peoples: "This one was born in Zion."

*Psalm 87:5-6*

*Thank You for establishing a dwelling place for me, Lord God.*

# AUGUST 7

¹³ But I cry to You for help, LORD; in the morning my prayer comes before You.
¹⁴ Why, LORD, do You reject me and hide Your face from me?

*Psalm 88:13-14*

*Lord, thank You for saving me and not rejecting me.*

# AUGUST 8

¹ I will sing of the LORD's great love forever; with my mouth I will make Your faithfulness known through all generations.
² I will declare that Your love stands firm forever, that You have established Your faithfulness in heaven itself.
³ You said, "I have made a covenant with my chosen one, I have sworn to David my servant,
⁴ 'I will establish your line forever and make your throne firm through all generations.'"

*Psalm 89:1-4*

*Lord, thank You for Your firm love and the reasons that I have faith.*

# AUGUST 9

[13] Relent, LORD! How long will it be? Have compassion on Your servants.
[14] Satisfy us in the morning with Your unfailing love, that we may sing for joy and be glad all our days.
[15] Make us glad for as many days as You have afflicted us, for as many years as we have seen trouble.
[16] May Your deeds be shown to Your servants, Your splendor to their children.
[17] May the favor of the Lord our God rest on us; establish the work of our hands for us—yes, establish the work of our hands.

*Psalm 90:13-17*

*Because of Your favor, Lord Our God, You have established the work of my hands and the path of my steps.*

# AUGUST 10

¹ Whoever dwells in the shelter of the Most High
   will rest in the shadow of the Almighty.
² I will say of the LORD, "He is my refuge and my fortress,
   my God, in whom I trust."

*Psalm 91:1-2*

**Lord, I trust You to make my dwelling place the Most High.**

# AUGUST 11

¹² The righteous will flourish like a palm tree, they will grow like a cedar of Lebanon;
¹³ planted in the house of the LORD, they will flourish in the courts of our God.
¹⁴ They will still bear fruit in old age, they will stay fresh and green,
¹⁵ proclaiming, "The LORD is upright; He is my Rock, and there is no wickedness in Him."

*Psalm 92:12-15*

*Between Your love, faith and deeds, Your love and Your thoughts, Lord, You overwhelm me, my heart and my mind.*

# AUGUST 12

¹ The LORD reigns, He is robed in majesty;
   the LORD is robed in majesty and armed with strength;
   indeed, the world is established, firm and secure.
² Your throne was established long ago;
   You are from all eternity.

*Psalm 93:1-2*

___

*Lord, You are holy and mighty!*

# AUGUST 13

²² But the LORD has become my fortress,
   and my God the rock in whom I take refuge.
²³ He will repay them for their sins
   and destroy them for their wickedness;
   the LORD our God will destroy them.

*Psalm 94:22-23*

_____
_____
_____
_____
_____
_____
_____
_____
_____
_____
_____
_____
_____
_____
_____
_____
_____
_____
_____
_____
_____
_____
_____
_____
_____

***Lord, for Your mercy and Your discipline, Your love and provision, I thank You.***

On This Journey

# AUGUST 14

³ For the LORD is the great God,
   the great King above all gods.
⁴ In His hand are the depths of the earth,
   and the mountain peaks belong to Him.
⁵ The sea is His, for He made it,
   and His hands formed the dry land.
⁶ Come, let us bow down in worship,
   let us kneel before the LORD our Maker;
⁷ for He is our God
   and we are the people of His pasture,
   the flock under His care.

*Psalm 95:3-7*

*Lord, please do not let my heart go astray.*

# AUGUST 15

[4] For great is the LORD and most worthy of praise;
   He is to be feared above all gods.
[5] For all the gods of the nations are idols,
   but the LORD made the heavens.
[6] Splendor and majesty are before Him;
   strength and glory are in His sanctuary.

*Psalm 96:4-6*

*For great are You, Lord, and worthy to be praised.*

# AUGUST 16

⁹ For You, LORD, are the Most High over all the earth;
   You are exalted far above all gods.
¹⁰ Let those who love the LORD hate evil,
   for He guards the lives of his faithful ones
   and delivers them from the hand of the wicked.
¹¹ Light shines on the righteous
   and joy on the upright in heart.
¹² Rejoice in the LORD, You who are righteous,
   and praise His holy name.

*Psalm 97:9-12*

_____

**Lord, do not let me trod in Your territory where You designate others to serve.**

# AUGUST 17

[1] Sing to the LORD a new song, for He has done marvelous things; His right hand and His holy arm have worked salvation for Him.
[2] The LORD has made His salvation known and revealed His righteousness to the nations.
[3] He has remembered His love and His faithfulness to Israel; all the ends of the earth have seen the salvation of our God.
[4] Shout for joy to the LORD, all the earth, burst into jubilant song with music;
[5] make music to the LORD with the harp, with the harp and the sound of singing,
[6] with trumpets and the blast of the ram's horn—shout for joy before the LORD, the King.

*Psalm 98:1-6*

*Thank You Lord for remembering me. I need Your favor.*

# AUGUST 18

⁸ LORD our God, You answered them; You were to Israel a forgiving God, though You punished their misdeeds.
⁹ Exalt the LORD, Our God and worship at His holy mountain, for the LORD, Our God is holy.

*Psalm 99:8-9*

*I owe You worship God because You created the definition of holy.*

# AUGUST 19

¹ Shout for joy to the LORD, all the earth.
² Worship the LORD with gladness;
  come before Him with joyful songs.
³ Know that the LORD is God.
  It is He who made us, and we are His;
  we are His people, the sheep of His pasture.
⁴ Enter His gates with thanksgiving and His courts with praise;
  give thanks to Him and praise His name.
⁵ For the LORD is good and His love endures forever;
  His faithfulness continues through all generations.

*Psalm 100*

*You made me, God, and not me myself, and for that I offer You my praise, worship, gratefulness, and love to You.*

# AUGUST 20

¹ I will sing of Your love and justice; to You, LORD, I will sing praise.
² I will be careful to lead a blameless life—when will You come to me?
 I will conduct the affairs of my house with a blameless heart.
³ I will not look with approval on anything that is vile.
 I hate what faithless people do; I will have no part in it.
⁴ The perverse of heart shall be far from me; I will have nothing to do with what is evil.

*Psalm 101:1-4*

**I sing my praises to God!**

# AUGUST 21

[1] Hear my prayer, LORD; let my cry for help come to You.
[2] Do not hide Your face from me when I am in distress.
Turn Your ear to me; when I call, answer me quickly.

*Psalm 102:1-2*

**Lord, please hear my prayer.**

# AUGUST 22

¹Bless the LORD, O my soul: and all that is within me, bless His holy name.
² Bless the LORD, O my soul, and forget not all His benefits:

*Psalm 103:1-2*

*Bless the Lord, oh my soul and all that is within me will bless His holy name.*

# AUGUST 23

[31] May the glory of the LORD endure forever; may the LORD rejoice in His works—
[32] He who looks at the earth, and it trembles, who touches the mountains, and they smoke.
[33] I will sing to the LORD all my life; I will sing praise to my God as long as I live.
[34] May my meditation be pleasing to Him, as I rejoice in the LORD.
[35] But may sinners vanish from the earth and the wicked be no more.
Praise the LORD, my soul.
Praise the LORD.

*Psalm 104:31-35*

*Father, I owe You both glory and honor because You are God and God alone.*

# AUGUST 24

¹ Give praise to the LORD, proclaim His name; make known among the nations what He has done.
² Sing to Him, sing praise to Him; tell of all His wonderful acts.
³ Glory in His holy name; let the hearts of those who seek the LORD rejoice.
⁴ Look to the LORD and His strength; seek His face always.

*Psalm 105:1-4*

*I will make known among nations what You have done for me and others, Father God.*

# AUGUST 25

[1] Praise the LORD.
Give thanks to the LORD, for He is good; His love endures forever.
[2] Who can proclaim the mighty acts of the LORD or fully declare His praise?
[3] Blessed are those who act justly, who always do what is right.

*Psalm 106:1-3*

*I am thankful for You God—for Your ever enduring love and Your mighty acts.*

# AUGUST 26

¹ Give thanks to the LORD, for He is good;
   His love endures forever.
² Let the redeemed of the LORD tell their story—
   those He redeemed from the hand of the foe,
³ those He gathered from the lands,
   from east and west, from north and south.

*Psalm 107:1-3*

*Lord, as a member of the redeemed, I will say so and share my story. No excuses going forward.*

# AUGUST 27

> [3] I will praise You, LORD, among the nations;
> I will sing of You among the peoples.
> [4] For great is Your love, higher than the heavens;
> Your faithfulness reaches to the skies.
> [5] Be exalted, O God, above the heavens;
> let Your glory be over all the earth.
>
> *Psalm 108:3-5*

**Lord, thank You for securing the victory for me!**

# AUGUST 28

¹ My God, whom I praise, do not remain silent,
² for people who are wicked and deceitful have opened their mouths against me;
they have spoken against me with lying tongues.
³ With words of hatred they surround me; they attack me without cause.
⁴ In return for my friendship they accuse me, but I am a man of prayer.
⁵ They repay me evil for good, and hatred for my friendship.
³⁰ With my mouth I will greatly extol the LORD; in the great throng of worshipers I will praise Him.
³¹ For He stands at the right hand of the needy, to save their lives from those who would condemn them.

*Psalm 109:1-5, 30-31*

**Lord, I am a person who prays. Hear me. Answer me.**

# AUGUST 29

[1] The LORD says to my lord:
"Sit at My right hand until I make your enemies a footstool for your feet."
[2] The LORD will extend your mighty scepter from Zion, saying, "Rule in the midst of your enemies!"

*Psalm 110:1-2*

_____
_____
_____
_____
_____
_____
_____
_____
_____
_____
_____
_____
_____
_____
_____
_____
_____
_____
_____
_____
_____
_____
_____
_____
_____
_____
_____

*Lord Almighty, I will sit still until You make my enemies my footstool.*

# AUGUST 30

¹ Praise the LORD.
I will extol the LORD with all my heart in the council of the upright and in the assembly.
² Great are the works of the LORD; they are pondered by all who delight in them.
³ Glorious and majestic are His deeds, and His righteousness endures forever.
⁴ He has caused His wonders to be remembered; the LORD is gracious and compassionate.
⁵ He provides food for those who fear Him; He remembers His covenant forever.
¹⁰ The fear of the LORD is the beginning of wisdom; all who follow His precepts have good understanding. To Him belongs eternal praise.

*Psalm 111:1-5, 10*

*Lord, I fear You so that makes me noise. I will give You my eternal praise.*

# AUGUST 31

⁶ Surely the righteous will never be shaken; they will be remembered forever.
⁷ They will have no fear of bad news; their hearts are steadfast, trusting in the LORD.
⁸ Their hearts are secure, they will have no fear; in the end they will look in triumph on their foes.
⁹ They have freely scattered their gifts to the poor, their righteousness endures forever;
  their horn will be lifted high in honor.

*Psalm 112:6-9*

*Father, I will praise You.*

# SEPTEMBER 1

> [4] The LORD is exalted over all the nations,
>   His glory above the heavens.
> [5] Who is like the LORD our God,
>   the One who sits enthroned on high,
> [6] who stoops down to look
>   on the heavens and the earth?
>
> *Psalm 113:4-6*

**Lord, I will praise You without being bribed.**

# SEPTEMBER 2

[7] Tremble, earth, at the presence of the Lord,
   at the presence of the God of Jacob,
[8] who turned the rock into a pool,
   the hard rock into springs of water.

*Psalm 114:7-8*

_____
_____
_____
_____
_____
_____
_____
_____
_____
_____
_____
_____
_____
_____
_____
_____
_____
_____
_____
_____
_____
_____
_____
_____
_____
_____
_____
_____

**Lord, I am in awe of You.**

# SEPTEMBER 3

<sup>16</sup> The highest heavens belong to the LORD,
  but the earth he has given to mankind.
<sup>17</sup> It is not the dead who praise the LORD,
  those who go down to the place of silence;
<sup>18</sup> it is we who extol the LORD,
  both now and forevermore.
Praise the LORD.

*Psalm 115:16-18*

*Father, to Your name be the honor and glory.*

# SEPTEMBER 4

¹ I love the LORD, for He heard my voice;
   He heard my cry for mercy.
² Because He turned His ear to me,
   I will call on Him as long as I live.
³ The cords of death entangled me, the anguish of the grave came over me;
   I was overcome by distress and sorrow.
⁴ Then I called on the name of the LORD:
   "LORD, save me!"
⁵ The LORD is gracious and righteous;
   our God is full of compassion.
⁶ The LORD protects the unwary;
   when I was brought low, He saved me.

*1 Thessalonians 4:12*

*I love You, Lord, for You hear my voice.*

On This Journey

# SEPTEMBER 5

[1] Praise the LORD, all you nations;
 extol Him, all you peoples.
[2] For great is His love toward us,
 and the faithfulness of the LORD endures forever.
Praise the LORD.

*Psalm 117*

*Lord, Your love is great towards me.*

# SEPTEMBER 6

<sup>26</sup> Blessed is he who comes in the name of the LORD.
　From the house of the LORD we bless You.
<sup>27</sup> The LORD is God,
　and He has made His light shine on us.
　With boughs in hand, join in the festal procession
　up to the horns of the altar.
<sup>28</sup> You are my God, and I will praise You;
　You are my God, and I will exalt You.
<sup>29</sup> Give thanks to the LORD, for He is good;
　His love endures forever.

*Psalm 118:26-29*

**Lord, Your love for me outlasts my Earthly existence.**

# SEPTEMBER 7

[10] I seek You with all my heart;
do not let me stray from Your commands.
[11] I have hidden Your word in my heart
that I might not sin against You.
[105] Your word is a lamp for my feet,
a light on my path.
[106] I have taken an oath and confirmed it,
that I will follow Your righteous laws.
[107] I have suffered much;
preserve my life, LORD, according to Your word.
[108] Accept, LORD, the willing praise of my mouth,
and teach me Your laws.
[109] Though I constantly take my life in my hands,
I will not forget Your law.
[110] The wicked have set a snare for me,
but I have not strayed from Your precepts.
[111] Your statutes are my heritage forever;
they are the joy of my heart.
[112] My heart is set on keeping your decrees
to the very end.

*Psalm 119:10-11, 105-112*

**Lord, I have Your word hidden in my heart and hopefully I can remember it when I need it. I am going to use the light You supply for me to make my paths clear.**

# SEPTEMBER 8

<sup>1</sup> I call on the LORD in my distress,
   and He answers me.
<sup>2</sup> Save me, LORD,
   from lying lips
   and from deceitful tongues.
<sup>6</sup> Too long have I lived
   among those who hate peace.
<sup>7</sup> I am for peace;
   but when I speak, they are for war.

*Psalm 120:1-2, 6-7*

**Lord, help me establish peace according to Your will.**

# SEPTEMBER 9

¹ I lift up my eyes to the mountains—
 where does my help come from?
² My help comes from the LORD,
 the Maker of heaven and earth.
³ He will not let your foot slip—
 He who watches over you will not slumber;
⁴ indeed, He who watches over Israel
 will neither slumber nor sleep.
⁵ The LORD watches over you—
 the LORD is your shade at your right hand;
⁶ the sun will not harm you by day,
 nor the moon by night.
⁷ The LORD will keep you from all harm—
 He will watch over your life;
⁸ the LORD will watch over your coming and going
 both now and forevermore.

*Psalm 121*

*Lord, I know that I am to call on You in my time of need and trouble.*

# SEPTEMBER 10

⁶ Pray for the peace of Jerusalem:
  "May those who love you be secure.
⁷ May there be peace within your walls
  and security within your citadels."
⁸ For the sake of my family and friends,
  I will say, "Peace be within you."
⁹ For the sake of the house of the LORD our God,
  I will seek your prosperity.

*Psalm 122:6-9*

---

**Lord, I rejoice when it is time to come to the house of the Lord.**

# SEPTEMBER 11

¹ I lift up my eyes to You, to You who sit enthroned in heaven.
² As the eyes of slaves look to the hand of their master,
　as the eyes of a female slave look to the hand of her mistress,
　so our eyes look to the LORD our God, till He shows us His mercy.
³ Have mercy on us, LORD, have mercy on us,
　for we have endured no end of contempt.
⁴ We have endured no end of ridicule from the arrogant, of contempt from the proud.

*Psalm 123*

***Father, help me keep my eyes stayed on You.***

# SEPTEMBER 12

⁶ Praise be to the LORD,
  who has not let us be torn by their teeth.
⁷ We have escaped like a bird from the fowler's snare;
  the snare has been broken, and we have escaped.
⁸ Our help is in the name of the LORD,
  the Maker of heaven and earth.

*Psalm 124:6-8*

*Maker, thank You for being on my side.*

# SEPTEMBER 13

⁴ LORD, do good to those who are good,
   to those who are upright in heart.
⁵ But those who turn to crooked ways
   the LORD will banish with the evildoers.
Peace be on Israel.

*Psalm 125:4-5*

*Jehovah, let me not be an evil doer. I do not want to meet Your wrath.*

Prayer Jornnal for Young People

# SEPTEMBER 14

[1] When the LORD restored the fortunes of Zion, we were like those who dreamed.
[2] Our mouths were filled with laughter, our tongues with songs of joy.
Then it was said among the nations, "The LORD has done great things for them."
[3] The LORD has done great things for us, and we are filled with joy.

*Psalm 126:1-3*

*Thank You, Father for the great things that You have done.*

MINISTER GAGE

# SEPTEMBER 15

[1] Unless the LORD builds the house, the builders labor in vain.
Unless the LORD watches over the city, the guards stand watch in vain.
[2] In vain you rise early and stay up late, toiling for food to eat—
   for He grants sleep to those He loves.
[3] Children are a heritage from the LORD,
   offspring a reward from Him.

*Psalm 127:1-3*

**Lord, You are the builder of my life and all my natural possession. Please help.**

# SEPTEMBER 16

[1] Blessed are all who fear the LORD,
 who walk in obedience to him.
[2] You will eat the fruit of your labor;
 blessings and prosperity will be yours.

*Psalm 128:1-2*

*Fear and obedience are imperative to a great relationship with You, God. Please help.*

## SEPTEMBER 17

¹ "They have greatly oppressed me from my youth," let Israel say;
² "they have greatly oppressed me from my youth, but they have not gained the victory over me.
³ Plowmen have plowed my back and made their furrows long.
⁴ But the LORD is righteous; He has cut me free from the cords of the wicked."

*Psalm 129:1-4*

*Thank You for cutting the cord from the wicked, Lord God.*

# SEPTEMBER 18

¹ Out of the depths I cry to You, LORD;
² Lord, hear my voice.
  Let Your ears be attentive to my cry for mercy.
³ If You, LORD, kept a record of sins, Lord, who could stand?
⁴ But with You there is forgiveness, so that we can, with reverence, serve You.
⁵ I wait for the LORD, my whole being waits, and in His word I put my hope.
⁶ I wait for the Lord more than watchmen wait for the morning,
  more than watchmen wait for the morning.
⁷ Israel, put your hope in the LORD, for with the LORD is unfailing love
  and with Him is full redemption.
⁸ He Himself will redeem Israel from all their sins.

*Psalm 130*

**Lord, I am crying to You and I need Your attention.**

# SEPTEMBER 19

[1] My heart is not proud, LORD, my eyes are not haughty;
I do not concern myself with great matters or things too wonderful for me.
[2] But I have calmed and quieted myself, I am like a weaned child with its mother;
like a weaned child I am content.
[3] Israel, put your hope in the LORD both now and forevermore.

*Psalm 131*

*Lord, I am not proud or haughty. Help me remain humble.*

# SEPTEMBER 20

¹¹ The LORD swore an oath to David, a sure oath He will not revoke:
"One of your own descendants I will place on your throne.
¹² If your sons keep my covenant and the statutes I teach them,
then their sons will sit on your throne for ever and ever."

*Psalm 132:11-12*

**Lord, help me keep my word.**

# SEPTEMBER 21

[1] How good and pleasant it is when God's people live together in unity!
[2] It is like precious oil poured on the head, running down on the beard, running down on Aaron's beard, down on the collar of his robe.
[3] It is as if the dew of Hermon were falling on Mount Zion.
For there the LORD bestows his blessing, even life forevermore.

*Psalm 133*

*Master, help me to be a unifying force.*

# SEPTEMBER 22

¹ Praise the LORD, all you servants of the LORD
  who minister by night in the house of the LORD.
² Lift up your hands in the sanctuary
  and praise the LORD.
³ May the LORD bless you from Zion,
  he who is the Maker of heaven and earth.

*Psalm 134*

**Lord, I will praise and worship You at all times.**

# SEPTEMBER 23

¹ Praise the LORD. Praise the name of the LORD; praise Him, you servants of the LORD,
² you who minister in the house of the LORD,
  in the courts of the house of our God.
³ Praise the LORD, for the LORD is good;
  sing praise to His name, for that is pleasant.
⁴ For the LORD has chosen Jacob to be His own,
  Israel to be His treasured possession.
⁵ I know that the LORD is great,
  that our Lord is greater than all gods.
⁶ The LORD does whatever pleases Him,
  in the heavens and on the earth, in the seas and all their depths.

*Psalm 135:1-6*

*Praise for You, Lord cannot be selective.*

# SEPTEMBER 24

¹ Give thanks to the LORD, for He is good.
*His love endures forever.*
² Give thanks to the God of gods.
*His love endures forever.*
³ Give thanks to the Lord of lords:
*His love endures forever.*
⁴ to him who alone does great wonders,
*His love endures forever.*
⁵ who by His understanding made the heavens,
*His love endures forever.*
⁶ who spread out the earth upon the waters,
*His love endures forever.*

*Psalm 136:1-6*

**Thank You for being good and enduring forever, Lord.**

# SEPTEMBER 25

⁴ How can we sing the songs of the LORD while in a foreign land?
⁵ If I forget you, Jerusalem, may my right hand forget its skill.
⁶ May my tongue cling to the roof of my mouth if I do not remember you, if I do not consider Jerusalem my highest joy.

*Psalm 137:4-6*

**Lord, I will remember to praise You when You bless me.**

Prayer Jornnal for Young People

# SEPTEMBER 26

[6] Though the LORD is exalted, he looks kindly on the lowly; though lofty, He sees them from afar.
[7] Though I walk in the midst of trouble, You preserve my life. You stretch out Your hand against the anger of my foes; with Your right hand You save me.
[8] The LORD will vindicate me; Your love, LORD, endures forever—do not abandon the works of Your hands.

*Psalm 138:6-8*

*With all my heart, Lord, I will praise You.*

# SEPTEMBER 27

¹ You have searched me, LORD, and You know me.
² You know when I sit and when I rise; You perceive my thoughts from afar.
³ You discern my going out and my lying down; You are familiar with all my ways.
⁴ Before a word is on my tongue You, LORD, know it completely.
⁵ You hem me in behind and before, and You lay Your hand upon me.
⁶ Such knowledge is too wonderful for me, too lofty for me to attain.
⁷ Where can I go from Your Spirit? Where can I flee from Your presence?
⁸ If I go up to the heavens, You are there; if I make my bed in the depths, You are there.
⁹ If I rise on the wings of the dawn, if I settle on the far side of the sea,
¹⁰ even there Your hand will guide me, Your right hand will hold me fast.
¹¹ If I say, "Surely the darkness will hide me and the light become night around me,"
¹² even the darkness will not be dark to You; the night will shine like the day, for darkness is as light to You.
¹³ For You created my inmost being; You knit me together in my mother's womb.
¹⁴ I praise You because I am fearfully and wonderfully made; Your works are wonderful, I know that full well.

*Psalm 139:1-14*

**Lord, You know me better than I know myself; I praise You because I am fearfully and wonderfully made.**

# SEPTEMBER 28

[4] Keep me safe, LORD, from the hands of the wicked; protect me from the violent, who devise ways to trip my feet.
[5] The arrogant have hidden a snare for me; they have spread out the cords of their net and have set traps for me along my path.
[6] I say to the LORD, "You are my God." Hear, LORD, my cry for mercy.
[7] Sovereign LORD, my strong deliverer, You shield my head in the day of battle.
[8] Do not grant the wicked their desires, LORD; do not let their plans succeed.

*Psalm 140:4-8*

*Sovereign God, You are my deliverer and my strong tower.*

# SEPTEMBER 29

³ Set a guard over my mouth, LORD; keep watch over the door of my lips.
⁴ Do not let my heart be drawn to what is evil so that I take part in wicked deeds along with those who are evildoers; do not let me eat their delicacies.
⁸ But my eyes are fixed on You, Sovereign LORD; in You I take refuge—do not give me over to death.
⁹ Keep me safe from the traps set by evildoers, from the snares they have laid for me.
¹⁰ Let the wicked fall into their own nets, while I pass by in safety.

*Psalm 141:3-4, 8-10*

*My eyes and heart are fixed on You, Sovereign Lord.*

# SEPTEMBER 30

¹ I cry aloud to the LORD; I lift up my voice to the LORD for mercy.
² I pour out before Him my complaint; before Him I tell my trouble.
³ When my spirit grows faint within me, it is You who watch over my way. In the path where I walk people have hidden a snare for me.
⁴ Look and see, there is no one at my right hand; no one is concerned for me. I have no refuge; no one cares for my life.
⁵ I cry to you, LORD; I say, "You are my refuge, my portion in the land of the living."
⁶ Listen to my cry, for I am in desperate need; rescue me from those who pursue me, for they are too strong for me.
⁷ Set me free from my prison, that I may praise Your name. Then the righteous will gather about me because of Your goodness to me.

*Psalm 142*

*Lord, I know that You want me to praise, worship and serve You whatever the condition.*

On This Journey

# READING GOD'S WORD

When you've heard your pastor or parents or other leaders say something and you thought 'wow', have you ever wondered how could they say that or know that or where did they get that from? Sure, we do. When I hear something of that magnitude, I look for it in God's word now. They can use God's word because they know God's words. They study the Bible and they read the Bible. They also realize that the Bible covers all subjects.

"How do I know what God's words say?" Read. Read. Read. Study. Study. Study. You must set aside time to read and study the Bible. If you start with 10-15 minutes per day, then you will increase that as you yearn more for His word.

"Where to start?" My suggestions are my favorite books: Matthew, Ephesians, James and Proverbs. Starting in any of these books will be easy. These books are an easy to read and understand. They also offer insight into your daily living and answers to your questions. Some books of the Bible require note taking, for me, especially with the names for ancestry and lineage. The history books of the Bible offer us information to understand the New Testament. The New Testament is not difficult but the more background you have, the better you will understand and deeper the meaning will be. For example, the prophets spoke of Jesus' birth, death and resurrection in the Old Testament. When He is born in the New Testament, John refers to the prophets of the Old Testament who spoke of His birth. Knowing this deepens your understanding for God's omniscience and omnipotence. Your knowledge will drive you to more knowledge. The more I know, the more I want to know.

"How do I find those great and special scriptures they know?" Spend time getting to know your sword (Ephesians 6:17). There are tools in your Sword to assist you in your study. The Bible has a table of contents and a key to assist you to understand the symbols used throughout the scriptures. In the front of each book, there is information and history given to clarify and provide background for the book. Included is usually a glossary and a concordance or index. The index allows you to use topics to find all scriptures related to the topic. There also some other quick reference resources, which assist you in answering your questions. These Bible helps are easy to follow and easy to use. You need to be consistent with your use.

Once you have read some more scripture, then you need to select a few scriptures to memorize. You memorize them by reading aloud, writing and repeating. Then apply it to your life, which will help you remember the scripture. Just a note, I once thought I couldn't remember scripture, but then I realized that I know the words to at least 50 songs, both Christian and secular, all of which are longer than a scripture.

It will help you to read more when you have a study partner. You will have accountability to your partner and vice versa. Spend time with His word. It's well worth your time.

God requires a tenth of what He has given us, so we have 2 hours and 24 minutes we owe to God daily. That time should be shared between reading and praying.

# OCTOBER 1

[7] Answer me quickly, LORD; my spirit fails. Do not hide Your face from me or I will be like those who go down to the pit.
[8] Let the morning bring me word of Your unfailing love, for I have put my trust in You. Show me the way I should go, for to You I entrust my life.
[9] Rescue me from my enemies, LORD, for I hide myself in You.
[10] Teach me to do Your will, for you are my God; may Your good Spirit lead me on level ground.
[11] For Your name's sake, LORD, preserve my life; in Your righteousness, bring me out of trouble.
[12] In Your unfailing love, silence my enemies; destroy all my foes, for I am Your servant.

*Psalm 143:7-12*

*Until You rescued me God, I thought the enemy had defeated me.*

# OCTOBER 2

¹ Praise be to the LORD my Rock, who trains my hands for war, my fingers for battle.
² He is my loving God and my fortress, my stronghold and my deliverer, my shield, in whom I take refuge, who subdues peoples under me.
³ LORD, what are human beings that You care for them, mere mortals that You think of them?
⁴ They are like a breath; their days are like a fleeting shadow.
⁵ Part Your heavens, LORD, and come down; touch the mountains, so that they smoke.
⁶ Send forth lightning and scatter the enemy; shoot Your arrows and rout them.

*Psalm 144:1-6*

*Blessed am I because You are my God.*

# OCTOBER 3

¹ I will exalt You, my God the King;
  I will praise Your name for ever and ever.
² Every day I will praise You
  and extol Your name for ever and ever.
³ Great is the LORD and most worthy of praise;
  His greatness no one can fathom.
⁴ One generation commends Your works to another;
  they tell of Your mighty acts.
⁵ They speak of the glorious splendor of Your majesty—
  and I will meditate on Your wonderful works.
⁶ They tell of the power of Your awesome works—
  and I will proclaim Your great deeds.
⁷ They celebrate Your abundant goodness
  and joyfully sing of Your righteousness.
⁸ The LORD is gracious and compassionate,
  slow to anger and rich in love.

*Psalm 145:1-8*

**Lord, my mouth and my heart will praise You and not curse You.**

# OCTOBER 4

[1] Praise the LORD. Praise the LORD, my soul.
[2] I will praise the LORD all my life;
   I will sing praise to my God as long as I live.
[3] Do not put your trust in princes,
   in human beings, who cannot save.
[4] When their spirit departs, they return to the ground;
   on that very day their plans come to nothing.
[5] Blessed are those whose help is the God of Jacob,
   whose hope is in the LORD their God.
[6] He is the Maker of heaven and earth,
   the sea, and everything in them—
   he remains faithful forever.

*Psalm 146:1-6*

*Thank You Father for the miracles You perform in my life, the protection You provide and Your sustaining power.*

# OCTOBER 5

[1] Praise the LORD. How good it is to sing praises to our God, how pleasant and fitting to praise Him!
[2] The LORD builds up Jerusalem; He gathers the exiles of Israel.
[3] He heals the brokenhearted and binds up their wounds.
[4] He determines the number of the stars and calls them each by name.
[5] Great is our Lord and mighty in power; His understanding has no limit.
[6] The LORD sustains the humble but casts the wicked to the ground.

*Psalm 147:1-6*

**Lord, thank You for revealing Your word to me.**

# OCTOBER 6

¹³ Let them praise the name of the LORD,
   for His name alone is exalted;
   His splendor is above the earth and the heavens.
¹⁴ And He has raised up for His people a horn,
   the praise of all His faithful servants,
   of Israel, the people close to His heart.
Praise the LORD.

*Psalm 148:13-14*

*I will praise You, Lord.*

Prayer Jornnal for Young People

# OCTOBER 7

<sup>6</sup> May the praise of God be in their mouths
and a double-edged sword in their hands,
<sup>7</sup> to inflict vengeance on the nations
and punishment on the peoples,
<sup>8</sup> to bind their kings with fetters,
their nobles with shackles of iron,
<sup>9</sup> to carry out the sentence written against them—
this is the glory of all his faithful people.
Praise the LORD.

*Psalm 149:6-9*

*I just want to honor You. Thank You for taking delight in me.*

MINISTER GAGE

# OCTOBER 8

¹ Praise the LORD.
Praise God in His sanctuary;
    praise Him in His mighty heavens.
² Praise Him for His acts of power;
    praise Him for His surpassing greatness.
³ Praise Him with the sounding of the trumpet,
    praise Him with the harp and lyre,
⁴ praise Him with timbrel and dancing,
    praise Him with the strings and pipe,
⁵ praise Him with the clash of cymbals,
    praise Him with resounding cymbals.
⁶ Let everything that has breath praise the LORD.
Praise the LORD.

*Psalm 150*

*Thank You for the reminders and reasons for praising You, Lord.*

# OCTOBER 9

² Then the LORD replied:

"Write down the revelation and make it plain on tablets so that a herald may run with it. ³ For the revelation awaits an appointed time; it speaks of the end and will not prove false. Though it linger, wait for it; it will certainly come and will not delay.

*Habakkuk 2:2-3*

*Thank You for the discipline to write the vision You have created for me.*

# OCTOBER 10

> [3] "Blessed are the poor in spirit,
> for theirs is the kingdom of heaven.
>
> *Matthew 5:3*

**Lord, thank You for offering me the kingdom of heaven as a reward.**

# OCTOBER 11

[4] Blessed are those who mourn,
for they will be comforted.

*Matthew 5:4*

*Father, thank You for comforting me when I am mourning.*

# OCTOBER 12

⁵ Blessed are the meek,
for they will inherit the earth.

*Matthew 5:5*

*Father, show me how to be meek because I really want to inherit the Earth.*

# OCTOBER 13

⁶ Blessed are those who hunger and thirst for righteousness,
for they will be filled.

*Matthew 5:6*

*Master, thank You for causing my thirst and hunger for righteous and filling it as well.*

# OCTOBER 14

⁷ Blessed are the merciful,
for they will be shown mercy.

*Matthew 5:7*

*Please remind me Lord to be compassionate so that I can recognize when to be merciful to others. I certainly want mercy for myself.*

# OCTOBER 15

⁸ Blessed are the pure in heart,
for they will see God.

*Matthew 5:8*

*Father, help me to keep my heart pure because above all else I want to see You!*

# OCTOBER 16

> [9] Blessed are the peacemakers,
> for they will be called children of God.
>
> *Matthew 5:9*

*Lord, help me to remain peaceful even when others want otherwise.*

# OCTOBER 17

[10] Blessed are those who are persecuted because of righteousness, for theirs is the kingdom of heaven.

*Matthew 5:10*

---

*Lord, I take my freedom to worship and serve You for granted. There are Christians who do trying; continue to bless them.*

# OCTOBER 18

<sup></sup>11 "Blessed are you when people insult you, persecute you and falsely say all kinds of evil against you because of me. <sup></sup>12 Rejoice and be glad, because great is your reward in heaven, for in the same way they persecuted the prophets who were before you.

*Matthew 5:11-12*

*Father, sometimes I forget they insult me because of who I am to You and who You are to me. I needed that reminder because sometimes they even pose as Christians.*

# OCTOBER 19

[44] But I tell you, love your enemies and pray for those who persecute you,
[46] If you love those who love you, what reward will you get? Are not even the tax collectors doing that?

*Matthew 5:44, 46*

**Lord, I will try to do better about loving those who persecute me.**

# OCTOBER 20

⁹ "This, then, is how you should pray:

"'Our Father in heaven, hallowed be your name,
¹⁰ your kingdom come, your will be done,
   on earth as it is in heaven.
¹¹ Give us today our daily bread.
¹² And forgive us our debts,
   as we also have forgiven our debtors.
¹³ And lead us not into temptation,
   but deliver us from the evil one.'

*Matthew 6:9-13*

___

*Lord, I still weep when I say Your prayer!*

# OCTOBER 21

[16] "When you fast, do not look somber as the hypocrites do, for they disfigure their faces to show others they are fasting. Truly I tell you, they have received their reward in full. [17] But when you fast, put oil on your head and wash your face, [18] so that it will not be obvious to others that you are fasting, but only to your Father, who is unseen; and your Father, who sees what is done in secret, will reward you.

*Matthew 6:16-18*

**Master, help me to fast more often.**

# OCTOBER 22

*31* "Simon, Simon, Satan has asked to sift all of you as wheat. *32* But I have prayed for you, Simon, that your faith may not fail. And when you have turned back, strengthen your brothers."

*Luke 22:31-32*

**Lord, I want You to say the next time Satan asks to sift me. I know that You won't, but I just thought I would ask. Thank You for the opportunity of increased faith and maturity.**

# OCTOBER 23

[34] Jesus answered, "I tell you, Peter, before the rooster crows today, you will deny three times that you know Me."

*Luke 22:34*

**Lord, I get so sad when I deny You. I apologize.**

# OCTOBER 24

[41] He withdrew about a stone's throw beyond them, knelt down and prayed,

*Luke 22:41*

*Lord, thank You for THE example of prayer.*

# OCTOBER 25

**8** Then Jesus said to him, "Get up! Pick up your mat and walk."

*John 5:8*

*Master, thank You for the command and the blessing of Your healing to go and do what You have equipped us to do.*

MINISTER GAGE

# OCTOBER 26

⁴ He fell to the ground and heard a voice say to him, "Saul, Saul, why do you persecute Me?" ⁵ "Who are You, Lord?" Saul asked. "I am Jesus, whom you are persecuting," He replied. ⁶ "Now get up and go into the city, and you will be told what you must do."

*Acts 9:4-6*

*Lord, I hope it never requires that much effort to get my attention.*

# OCTOBER 27

[20] At once he began to preach in the synagogues that Jesus is the Son of God. [21] All those who heard him were astonished and asked, "Isn't he the man who raised havoc in Jerusalem among those who call on This name? And hasn't he come here to take them as prisoners to the chief priests?"

*Acts 9:20-21*

***Father, help me keep an upright heart.***

# OCTOBER 28

[22] Yet Saul grew more and more powerful and baffled the Jews living in Damascus by proving that Jesus is the Messiah.

*Acts 9:22*

*Lord, forgive me and correct the unrighteousness in my heart. Create in me a clean heart.*

# OCTOBER 29

[27] And He who searches our hearts knows the mind of the Spirit, because the Spirit intercedes for God's people in accordance with the will of God.

*Romans 8:27*

*Lord, please align me with the Spirit who is aligned with You.*

# OCTOBER 30

²⁹ For those God foreknew He also predestined to be conformed to the image of His Son, that he might be the firstborn among many brothers and sisters. ³⁰ And those He predestined, He also called; those He called, h He e also justified; those He justified, He also glorified.

*Romans 8:29-30*

*Lord, You have given me so much and put me in amazing places because of Your name and image.*

# OCTOBER 31

<sup>35</sup> Who shall separate us from the love of Christ? Shall trouble or hardship or persecution or famine or nakedness or danger or sword?

*Romans 8:35*

*Lord, I hope that I never cause us to be separated. I love You and I desperately need Your love.*

# NOVEMBER 1

[37] No, in all these things we are more than conquerors through Him who loved us.

*Romans 8:37*

*Father, thank You for making me more than a conqueror.*

Prayer Jornnal for Young People

# NOVEMBER 2

[38] For I am convinced that neither death nor life, neither angels nor demons, neither the present nor the future, nor any powers, [39] neither height nor depth, nor anything else in all creation, will be able to separate us from the love of God that is in Christ Jesus our Lord.

*Romans 8:38-39*

**Lord, I will let nothing separate us from the love You have for me.**

MINISTER GAGE

# NOVEMBER 3

[1]If I speak in the tongues of men or of angels, but do not have love, I am only a resounding gong or a clanging cymbal.

*1 Corinthians 13:1*

---

**Lord, without love I am nothing. Sometimes, God I am nothing.**

# NOVEMBER 4

² If I have the gift of prophecy and can fathom all mysteries and all knowledge, and if I have a faith that can move mountains, but do not have love, I am nothing.

*1 Corinthians 13:2*

**Lord, sometimes I am nothing.**

# NOVEMBER 5

³ If I give all I possess to the poor and give over my body to hardship that I may boast, but do not have love, I gain nothing.

*1 Corinthians 13:3*

___

*Lord, sometimes I gain nothing.*

# NOVEMBER 6

[4] Love is patient, love is kind. It does not envy, it does not boast, it is not proud.

*1 Corinthians 13:4*

*Father, help me be love through patience, kindness, without envy, boasting, and pride.*

# NOVEMBER 7

[5] [Love] does not dishonor others, it is not self-seeking, it is not easily angered, it keeps no record of wrongs.

*1 Corinthians 13:5*

*Lord, help me to love more people.*

# NOVEMBER 8

⁶ Love does not delight in evil but rejoices with the truth.

*1 Corinthians 13:6*

*Lord, help me love more authentically.*

# NOVEMBER 9

[7] [Love] always protects, always trusts, always hopes, always perseveres.

*1 Corinthians 13:7*

*Lord, help me demonstrate love more consistently, by the use of Your definition.*

# NOVEMBER 10

[8] Love never fails. But where there are prophecies, they will cease; where there are tongues, they will be stilled; where there is knowledge, it will pass away.

*1 Corinthians 13:8*

*Lord, help me to love more consistently.*

# NOVEMBER 11

[9] For we know in part and we prophesy in part,

*1 Corinthians 13:9*

*Lord, help me to fulfill Your prophesy.*

# NOVEMBER 12

[10] but when completeness comes, what is in part disappears.

*1 Corinthians 13:10*

*Lord, help me be the definition of love Your created me to be.*

# NOVEMBER 13

[11] When I was a child, I talked like a child, I thought like a child, I reasoned like a child. When I became a man, I put the ways of childhood behind me.

*1 Corinthians 13:11*

*Father, help me refine my maturity.*

# NOVEMBER 14

¹² For now we see only a reflection as in a mirror; then we shall see face to face. Now I know in part; then I shall know fully, even as I am fully known.

*1 Corinthians 13:12*

**Lord, I cannot look in the mirror because I am not all that I am supposed to be.**

# NOVEMBER 15

¹³ But for right now, until that completeness, we have three things to do to lead us toward that consummation: Trust steadily in God, hope unswervingly, love extravagantly. And the best of the three is love.

*1 Corinthians 13:13 MSG*

**Lord, I want to love extravagantly without judgement or reservation.**

# NOVEMBER 16

⁶ I am astonished that you are so quickly deserting the one who called you to live in the grace of Christ and are turning to a different gospel—⁷ which is really no gospel at all. Evidently some people are throwing you into confusion and are trying to pervert the gospel of Christ.

*Galatians 1:6-7*

**God, there is ONE gospel—Yours!**

# NOVEMBER 17

¹¹ I want you to know, brothers and sisters, that the gospel I preached is not of human origin. ¹² I did not receive it from any man, nor was I taught it; rather, I received it by revelation from Jesus Christ.

***Galatians 1:11-12***

*Father, thank You for the revelation to give to me to teach and preach and proclaim the Gospel.*

# NOVEMBER 18

¹³ For you have heard of my previous way of life in Judaism, how intensely I persecuted the church of God and tried to destroy it. ¹⁴ I was advancing in Judaism beyond many of my own age among my people and was extremely zealous for the traditions of my fathers. ¹⁵ But when God, who set me apart from my mother's womb and called me by His grace, was pleased ¹⁶ to reveal His Son in me so that I might preach Him among the Gentiles, my immediate response was not to consult any human being.

*Galatians 1:13-16*

---

*Lord, remind me that Your calling on my life is for the advancement of Your ministry required that I do not consult another human being.*

# NOVEMBER 19

[14] For this reason I kneel before the Father,

*Ephesians 3:14*

*Lord, help me pray for others like Paul prayed for me.*

# NOVEMBER 20

¹⁵ from whom every family in heaven and on earth derives its name.

*Ephesians 3:15*

***Father, thank You for such a rich ancestry.***

# NOVEMBER 21

**16** I pray that out of His glorious riches He may strengthen you with power through his Spirit in your inner being,

*Ephesians 3:16*

*Father, thank You for the power in my inner being and help me access it better please.*

# NOVEMBER 22

[17] so that Christ may dwell in your hearts through faith. And I pray that you, being rooted and established in love,

*Ephesians 3:17*

*Father, I know that it is hard to dwell within me. Thank You for reminding me about the roots of Your love for me.*

# NOVEMBER 23

[18] may have power, together with all the Lord's holy people, to grasp how wide and long and high and deep is the love of Christ,

*Ephesians 3:18*

*God, that love for me which is high and wide and long and deep—infinite—thank You!*

# NOVEMBER 24

¹⁹ and to know this love that surpasses knowledge—that you may be filled to the measure of all the fullness of God.

*Ephesians 3:19*

*No, Lord, I do not understand why or how You love me so much.*

# NOVEMBER 25

[20] Now to Him who is able to do immeasurably more than all we ask or imagine, according to His power that is at work within us,

*Ephesians 3:20*

*Lord, I am now understanding the power at work within me and how You can only do what I am ready to receive and carry out.*

# NOVEMBER 26

[21] to Him be glory in the church and in Christ Jesus throughout all generations, for ever and ever! Amen.

*Ephesians 3:21*

*Thank You for exceeding my imagination and blessing the generations beyond me better than You blessed me.*

# NOVEMBER 27

[1]As a prisoner for the Lord, then, I urge you to live a life worthy of the calling you have received.

***Ephesians 4:1***

*Lord, help me to live a life worthy of Your calling on my life.*

# NOVEMBER 28

² Be completely humble and gentle; be patient, bearing with one another in love.

*Ephesians 4:2*

*Father, I do need more patience than others.*

# NOVEMBER 29

.[3] Make every effort to keep the unity of the Spirit through the bond of peace.

*Ephesians 4:3*

*Father, help me as I strive for unity and peace with others.*

# NOVEMBER 30

⁴ There is one body and one Spirit, just as you were called to one hope when you were called; ⁵ one Lord, one faith, one baptism; ⁶ one God and Father of all, who is over all and through all and in all.

*Ephesians 4:4-6*

**Lord, we are called to You: One Lord, One Faith, and One Baptism.**

# DECEMBER 1

¹¹ So Christ Himself gave the apostles, the prophets, the evangelists, the pastors and teachers, ¹² to equip His people for works of service, so that the body of Christ may be built up ¹³ until we all reach unity in the faith and in the knowledge of the Son of God and become mature, attaining to the whole measure of the fullness of Christ.

*Ephesians 4:11-13*

*Lord, I am gifted so that I can help advance Your Kingdom; help me!*

# DECEMBER 2

[17] So I tell you this, and insist on it in the Lord, that you must no longer live as the Gentiles do, in the futility of their thinking. [18] They are darkened in their understanding and separated from the life of God because of the ignorance that is in them due to the hardening of their hearts. [19] Having lost all sensitivity, they have given themselves over to sensuality so as to indulge in every kind of impurity, and they are full of greed.

*Ephesians 4:17-19*

*Father, keep my life pure, avoiding the temptation; keep me in the light, rather than the darkness that tends to draw me in. Lord, keep my heart pliable.*

# DECEMBER 3

[20] That, however, is not the way of life you learned [21] when you heard about Christ and were taught in him in accordance with the truth that is in Jesus. [22] You were taught, with regard to your former way of life, to put off your old self, which is being corrupted by its deceitful desires; [23] to be made new in the attitude of your minds; [24] and to put on the new self, created to be like God in true righteousness and holiness.

*Ephesians 4:20-24*

**Lord, You are calling me a new attitude and a new self in order to follow You better. I am willing.**

# DECEMBER 4

[10] Finally, be strong in the Lord and in His mighty power.

*Ephesians 6:10*

*Lord, I need to rely on You more, rather than thinking that I can do it alone.*

# DECEMBER 5

[11] Put on the full armor of God, so that you can take your stand against the devil's schemes.

***Ephesians 6:11***

*Lord, I will put on Your whole armor. I apology for neglecting pieces in the past.*

# DECEMBER 6

[12] For our struggle is not against flesh and blood, but against the rulers, against the authorities, against the powers of this dark world and against the spiritual forces of evil in the heavenly realms.

*Ephesians 6:12*

*Lord, give me a discerning spirit so that I will know when the evil spirits arrive.*

# DECEMBER 7

¹³ Therefore put on the full armor of God, so that when the day of evil comes, you may be able to stand your ground, and after you have done everything, to stand.

*Ephesians 6:13*

*Lord, thank You for the equipment to fight and the perseverance to stand against the evil one.*

# DECEMBER 8

[14] Stand firm then, with the belt of truth buckled around your waist, with the breastplate of righteousness in place,

*Ephesians 6:14*

*Lord, help me to tell the truth and be righteous.*

# DECEMBER 9

[15] and with your feet fitted with the readiness that comes from the gospel of peace.

*Ephesians 6:15*

**Lord, help me study the Gospel of Peace so that I can be more ready when issues arise.**

# DECEMBER 10

[16] In addition to all this, take up the shield of faith, with which you can extinguish all the flaming arrows of the evil one.

*Ephesians 6:16*

*Lord, my faith can extinguish the flaming arrows of the evil one. Help me keep it strong.*

# DECEMBER 11

[17] Take the helmet of salvation and the sword of the Spirit, which is the word of God.

***Ephesians 6:17***

***Father, thank You for the sword of the Spirit and the covering of Your salvation.***

# DECEMBER 12

[18] And pray in the Spirit on all occasions with all kinds of prayers and requests. With this in mind, be alert and always keep on praying for all of the Lord's people.

*Ephesians 6:18*

*Lord, help me to pray more.*

# DECEMBER 13

[19] Pray also for me, that whenever I speak, words may be given me so that I will fearlessly make known the mystery of the gospel, [20] for which I am an ambassador in chains. Pray that I may declare it fearlessly, as I should.

*Ephesians 6:19-20*

*Lord, help me to pray more for others.*

# DECEMBER 14

[1] You, however, must teach what is appropriate to sound doctrine. [2] Teach the older men to be temperate, worthy of respect, self-controlled, and sound in faith, in love and in endurance.

*Titus 2:1-2*

*Help me Father to learn sound doctrine so that I can teach more freely.*

# DECEMBER 15

³ Likewise, teach the older women to be reverent in the way they live, not to be slanderers or addicted to too much wine, but to teach what is good. ⁴ Then they can urge the younger women to love their husbands and children, ⁵ to be self-controlled and pure, to be busy at home, to be kind, and to be subject to their husbands, so that no one will malign the word of God.

*Titus 2:3-5*

*Lord, help me live a life that is an example for others so that they can be receptive to what I say.*

# DECEMBER 16

[6] Similarly, encourage the young men to be self-controlled. [7] In everything set them an example by doing what is good. In your teaching show integrity, seriousness [8] and soundness of speech that cannot be condemned, so that those who oppose you may be ashamed because they have nothing bad to say about us.

*Titus 2:6-8*

*Lord, let me live a life above reproach so that the words I share, which are Yours, can be received as intended.*

# DECEMBER 17

[3] By faith we understand that the universe was formed at God's command, so that what is seen was not made out of what was visible.

*Hebrews 11:3*

*Lord, help me upgrade my faith.*

# DECEMBER 18

⁴ By faith Abel brought God a better offering than Cain did. By faith he was commended as righteous, when God spoke well of his offerings. And by faith Abel still speaks, even though he is dead.

*Hebrews 11:4*

*Lord, I want to give You the best offering that I can!*

# DECEMBER 19

⁵ By faith Enoch was taken from this life, so that he did not experience death: "He could not be found, because God had taken him away." For before he was taken, he was commended as one who pleased God.

*Hebrews 11:5*

*Lord, I want to be commanded as someone who pleases You.*

Prayer Jornnal for Young People

# DECEMBER 20

⁶ And without faith it is impossible to please God, because anyone who comes to Him must believe that He exists and that He rewards those who earnestly seek Him.

*Hebrews 11:6*

*Lord, thank You for sharing how important my faith is to You.*

MINISTER GAGE

On This Journey

# DECEMBER 21

⁷ By faith Noah, when warned about things not yet seen, in holy fear built an ark to save his family. By his faith he condemned the world and became heir of the righteousness that is in keeping with faith.

*Hebrews 11:7*

*Lord, I want my faith to please You like Noah's did.*

# DECEMBER 22

[8] By faith Abraham, when called to go to a place he would later receive as his inheritance, obeyed and went, even though he did not know where he was going.

*Hebrews 11:8*

*Lord, help me to stop questioning You about my path.*

# DECEMBER 23

⁹ By faith he made his home in the promised land like a stranger in a foreign country; he lived in tents, as did Isaac and Jacob, who were heirs with him of the same promise.

*Hebrews 11:9*

*Lord, help me trust You when You send me anywhere.*

# DECEMBER 24

[10] For he was looking forward to the city with foundations, whose architect and builder is God.

*Hebrews 11:10*

*Help me Lord to find You when I seek You.*

# DECEMBER 25

[11] And by faith even Sarah, who was past childbearing age, was enabled to bear children because she considered him faithful who had made the promise.

*Hebrews 11:11*

*Lord, remind me that You keep Your promises based on my faith.*

# DECEMBER 26

[12] And so from this one man, and he as good as dead, came descendants as numerous as the stars in the sky and as countless as the sand on the seashore.

*Hebrews 11:12*

___

*Thank You Lord, for the descendants which will come from me, even after I am with You in Heaven.*

# DECEMBER 27

[17] By faith Abraham, when God tested him, offered Isaac as a sacrifice. He who had embraced the promises was about to sacrifice his one and only son, [18] even though God had said to him, "It is through Isaac that your offspring will be reckoned."

*Hebrews 11:17-18*

*Lord, I want to pass each test You give me, regardless of how hard.*

# DECEMBER 28

[21] By faith Jacob, when he was dying, blessed each of Joseph's sons, and worshiped as he leaned on the top of his staff.

*Hebrews 11:21*

**Lord, with faith, I can do all things.**

# DECEMBER 29

[39] These were all commended for their faith, yet none of them received what had been promised, [40] since God had planned something better for us so that only together with us would they be made perfect.

*Hebrews 11:39-40*

*Lord, help me have faith even when I do not receive what was promised.*

# DECEMBER 30

[1]Therefore, since we are surrounded by such a great cloud of witnesses, let us throw off everything that hinders and the sin that so easily entangles. And let us run with perseverance the race marked out for us, [2] fixing our eyes on Jesus, the pioneer and perfecter of faith. For the joy set before Him He endured the cross, scorning its shame, and sat down at the right hand of the throne of God. [3] Consider Him who endured such opposition from sinners, so that you will not grow weary and lose heart.

*Hebrews 12:1-3*

*Help me Father, when I want to stop and quit and lose heart and grow weary and sin!*

# DECEMBER 31

[2] Beloved, I pray that you may prosper in all things and be in health, just as your soul prospers.
*3 John 2 (NKJV)*

*Help me, Father, to keep my soul prospering.*

# DECEMBER 31.5

[3] It gave me great joy when some believers came and testified about your faithfulness to the truth, telling how you continue to walk in it. [4] I have no greater joy than to hear that my children are walking in the truth.

*3 John 3-4*

_____
_____
_____
_____
_____
_____
_____
_____
_____
_____
_____
_____
_____
_____
_____
_____
_____
_____
_____
_____
_____
_____
_____
_____
_____
_____

**Lord, I want to walk in truth and faith at all times.**

# GOD'S ANSWERS TO YOUR PRAYERS

As a young Christian, you will ask 'how will I know when God has answered me?' I know I did. I wanted to know God's plan, strategy and answers for me and my life and to my prayers. Through my growth, I have learned that God has three answers: yes, no and wait.

Yes means you are granted your request. God has designed this for you at this time. God knows He can trust you with your request. No means your request is denied because His plans and your request don't match at this time. God doesn't have this in plans for you. Sometimes, His plans have something different and better for you (i.e. He gives you a car but it's a practical one rather than a sports car) and other times no means He doesn't want you to have it at all.

Wait means you are not ready for your own request. He doesn't deny me, but He tells me I'm not prepared for the responsibilities of my request. If I am granted my request and am not ready then, I any misuse or mistreat my gift.

Thank Him as if your request has already been granted. Believe in your heart that God will grant your request and it will be yours. God's plans are better than any request you could ever so don't be disappointed when He says no or wait even. Ask with the purest of motives and your request has a better chance.

There is a note, which reads, "Ask God for what you want but willing to accept what He gives you because it will be better than what you ask for."

God will answer you. He never leaves a prayer unanswered. I wanted a new career so I pursued that career and was employed. There were a series of events which made me question why I left the previous employer if I was just going to return 90 days later. On September 11, 2001, God answered me. There were planes in buildings which were not supposed to be there. An incident we now refer to reverence as 9/11. If I had gotten my prayer request, I would have been in that building and it is likely that I would not have survived. Instead, I was home asleep when these unfortunate and tragic events occurred. I am blessed to be here and writing these documents. I am glad that God said no to my new career request. God offered me some relief, although temporary, but He really said no overall.

Prayer is a powerful tool by which God and us are giving each other our undivided attention. We are focused on Him. He promises to hear our plea. He promises us peace for our burdens and for those of us who are burdened and heavy-laden. He promises to meet our needs. He promises to give us the desires of our hearts. God expects, and quite frankly deserves, glory for all of His goodness. For all of His mercy and grace.

A word of caution: be careful of asking why when things don't go your way. God's answer could easily be 'why not you?' Events occur to determine whether or not we can be trusted with God's work and gifts. Job is one example of what can happen to us and the best example of how we are to respond when things do happen.

Do not lose heart. God is working in our lives at all times. When He determines we are ready, He answers our prayers.

On This Journey

# RESOURCES

# FOR

# THE JOURNEY

# THE NAMES OF GOD

| | |
|---|---|
| Elohim | The Creator |
| El Elyon | The God Most High |
| El Roi | God Who Sees |
| El Shaddai | The All-Sufficient One |
| Adonai | Lord, Master |
| Yahweh | Lord, Jehovah |
| Jehovah-jireh | The Lord Will Provide |
| Jehovah-rapha | The Lord That Healeth |
| Jehovah-nissi | The Lord My Banner |
| Jehovah-mekoddishkem | The Lord Who Sanctifies You |
| Jehovah-shalom | The Lord Is Peace |
| Jehovah-sabaoth | The Lord of Hosts |
| Jehovah-raah | The Lord My Shepherd |
| Jehovah-tsidkenu | The Lord Our Righteousness |
| Jehovah-shammah | The Lord is There |
| El Olam | The Everlasting God |

# THE PRAYER OF SALVATION

Salvation is defined by Random House as the act of saving or protecting from harm or loss. God provides salvation for us, His children, free of charge. In order to receive His salvation, we only have to accept Jesus as our Lord and Savior. Salvation is a gift, which we have nothing to earn and can do nothing to achieve. God planned salvation before He created each of us. The scriptures listed will show you God's plan and provision for your salvation. Then follows a prayer of salvation, which confesses your sin to God and will assist you in accepting God's gift of salvation.

| | |
|---|---|
| Romans 3:10-12, 23 | We are all sinners. |
| Romans 6:23 | The penalty for sin. |
| Romans 5:8-9 | The payment God made for sin. |
| Romans 10:9-10, 13 | Confess Jesus as Lord. |

Dear God: I know You love me. I realize I am a sinner. I have not lived as You have wanted me to live. I believe Your Son, Jesus, died for me on the cross and was raised from the dead to provide forgiveness and eternal life. Please save me as I turn from my sins, place my faith in Jesus and receive Him as Lord and Savior. I will no longer live according to my selfish desires and plans but will follow Your desires and plans for my life. Thank You for saving me and giving me eternal life. I pray this prayer in Jesus' name, Amen.

*What do I about my family and friends who are not saved?*
Your prayer for God to become Lord of their lives is critical. You have to pray for them diligently. You don't have to pushy. The Lord will handle the rest. You share with them what you know through your study and prayer and the Lord will do the rest. Invite them to your church. Don't be afraid to ask them about what they know and don't be afraid to share God with anyone, believers or not. Eventually, God will bring them to Him. Pray then watch Him work.

# ADDITIONAL SOURCES FOR THE JOURNEY

Disciple Youth Bible
True Love Waits Bible
Worth the Wait by Tim Stafford
Choosing God's Best by Dr. Don Raunikar
The Five Love Languages of Teenagers by Dr. Gary Chapman
The 7 Habits of Highly Effective Teens Sean Covey
Love Letters to God From a Teenage Girl by Onedia Gage
The Notebook for the Christian Teen by Onedia Gage

# INDEX

| | |
|---|---|
| Genesis 1:26—27 | 23 |
| Genesis 1:28—30 | 24 |
| Genesis 1:31 | 25 |
| Genesis 3:1 | 26 |
| Genesis 3:6—7 | 27 |
| Genesis 3:13—16 | 28 |
| Genesis 3:17—19 | 29 |
| Genesis 4:4—7 | 30 |
| Genesis 4:8—16 | 31 |
| Genesis 4:8—16 | 32 |
| Genesis 5 | 33 |
| Genesis 6:3 | 34 |
| Genesis 6:5—8 | 35 |
| Genesis 6:11—12 | 36 |
| Genesis 6:13, 17 | 37 |
| Genesis 6:14—16 | 38 |
| Genesis 6:18—21 | 39 |
| Genesis 6:22 | 40 |
| Genesis 7:11—12 | 41 |
| Genesis 7:17—21 | 42 |
| Genesis 7:22—23 | 43 |
| Genesis 7:24 | 44 |
| Genesis 8:21 | 45 |
| Genesis 9:12—17 | 46 |
| Genesis 15:1 | 47 |
| Genesis 15:6 | 48 |
| Genesis 37:3—4 | 49 |
| Genesis 37:5—8 | 50 |
| Genesis 37:9—10 | 51 |
| Genesis 37:11 | 52 |
| Genesis 37:18—22 | 53 |
| Genesis 37:23—25 | 54 |
| Genesis 37:26—29 | 55 |
| Genesis 37:22b, 29—30 | 56 |
| Genesis 37:31—33 | 57 |
| Genesis 37:34—35 | 58 |
| Genesis 37:36, 39:1 | 59 |
| Genesis 39:2—4 | 60 |
| Genesis 39:5—6 | 61 |
| Genesis 39:7—10 | 62 |
| Genesis 39:11—15 | 63 |
| Genesis 39:20—423 | 64 |
| Genesis 40 | 65 |
| Genesis 41:14—16 | 66 |
| Genesis 41:28—32 | 67 |
| Genesis 41:37—40 | 68 |
| Genesis 41:41—43 | 69 |
| Genesis 41:46 | 70 |
| Genesis 41:47—49 | 71 |
| Genesis 41:50—52 | 72 |
| Genesis 41:53—55 | 73 |
| Genesis 42:1—2 | 74 |
| Genesis 42:3—6 | 75 |
| Genesis 42:7—9 | 76 |
| Genesis 42:18—20 | 77 |
| Genesis 42:21 | 78 |
| Genesis 42:22—23 | 79 |
| Genesis 42:24 | 80 |
| Genesis 42:25—26 | 81 |
| Genesis 42:27—29 | 82 |
| Genesis 42:30—34 | 83 |
| Genesis 42:35 | 84 |
| Genesis 42:36 | 85 |
| Genesis 42:37—38 | 86 |
| Genesis 43:6—7 | 87 |
| Genesis 43:8—10 | 88 |
| Genesis 43:11—14 | 89 |
| Genesis 43:15—16 | 90 |
| Genesis 43:19—22 | 91 |
| Genesis 43:23 | 92 |
| Genesis 43:24—28 | 93 |
| Genesis 43:29—31 | 94 |
| Genesis 43:32—34 | 95 |
| Genesis 44:1—2 | 96 |
| Genesis 44:11—13 | 97 |
| Genesis 44:17 | 98 |
| Genesis 44:18—34 | 99 |
| Genesis 45:1—2 | 100 |
| Genesis 45:3—4 | 101 |
| Genesis 45:5 | 102 |
| Genesis 45:6—7 | 103 |
| Genesis 45:8—11 | 104 |
| Genesis 45:12—13 | 105 |
| Genesis 45:14—15 | 106 |

| | |
|---|---|
| Genesis 45:16—20 | 107 |
| Genesis 45:24 | 108 |
| Genesis 45:26—28 | 109 |
| Genesis 46:1—4 | 110 |
| Genesis 46:5—27 | 111 |
| Genesis 46:29 | 112, 129 |
| Genesis 46:30 | 113 |
| Genesis 47 | 115 |
| Genesis 48:15—22 | 116 |
| Genesis 50:15—19 | 117 |
| Genesis 50:20—21 | 118 |
| Genesis 50:22—26 | 119 |
| Deuteronomy 6:5 | 120 |
| Deuteronomy 6:6 | 121 |
| Deuteronomy 6:13 | 122 |
| Deuteronomy 6:18—19 | 123 |
| Joshua 1:7 | 124 |
| Joshua 1:9 | 125 |
| Joshua 4:21—24 | 126 |
| Ruth 1:16-17 | 127 |
| 1 Samuel 3:10 | 128 |
| 1 Samuel 16:7 | 129 |
| 1 Samuel 16:12 | 130 |
| 1 Samuel 17:33 | 131 |
| 1 Samuel 17:34—37 | 132 |
| 1 Samuel 17:38—39 | 133 |
| 1 Samuel 17:40—42 | 134 |
| 1 Samuel 17:45—47 | 135 |
| 1 Kings 2:2—4 | 136 |
| 1 Kings 3:3 | 137 |
| 1 Kings 3:6—9 | 138 |
| 1 Kings 3:10—14 | 139 |
| Job 1:8 | 140 |
| Job 1:9—11 | 141 |
| Job 1:12 | 142 |
| Job 1:20—21 | 143 |
| Job 1:22 | 144 |
| Job 2 | 146 |
| Job 4, 5 | 147 |
| Job 6, 7 | 148 |
| Job 8 | 149 |
| Job 37 | 150 |
| Job 38 | 151 |
| Job 39 | 152 |
| Job 40 | 153 |
| Job 41 | 154 |
| Job 42:1—6 | 155 |
| Job 42:10—17 | 156 |
| Psalm 1 | 157 |
| Psalm 2 | 158 |
| Psalm 3 | 159 |
| Psalm 4 | 160 |
| Psalm 5 | 161 |
| Psalm 6 | 162 |
| Psalm 7 | 163 |
| Psalm 8 | 164 |
| Psalm 9 | 165 |
| Psalm 10 | 166 |
| Psalm 11 | 167 |
| Psalm 12 | 168 |
| Psalm 13 | 169 |
| Psalm 14 | 170 |
| Psalm 15 | 171 |
| Psalm 16 | 172 |
| Psalm 17 | 173 |
| Psalm 18 | 174 |
| Psalm 19 | 175 |
| Psalm 20 | 176 |
| Psalm 21 | 177 |
| Psalm 22 | 178 |
| Psalm 23 | 179 |
| Psalm 24 | 180 |
| Psalm 25 | 181 |
| Psalm 26 | 182 |
| Psalm 27 | 183 |
| Psalm 28 | 184 |
| Psalm 29 | 185 |
| Psalm 30 | 186 |
| Psalm 31 | 187 |
| Psalm 32 | 188 |
| Psalm 33 | 189 |
| Psalm 34 | 190 |
| Psalm 35 | 191 |
| Psalm 36 | 192 |
| Psalm 37 | 193 |
| Psalm 38 | 194 |
| Psalm 39 | 195 |
| Psalm 40 | 196 |
| Psalm 41 | 197 |
| Psalm 42 | 198 |

| | | | |
|---|---|---|---|
| Psalm 43 | 199 | Psalm 88 | 245 |
| Psalm 44 | 200 | Psalm 89 | 246 |
| Psalm 45 | 201 | Psalm 90 | 247 |
| Psalm 46 | 202 | Psalm 91 | 248 |
| Psalm 47 | 203 | Psalm 92 | 249 |
| Psalm 48 | 204 | Psalm 93 | 250 |
| Psalm 49 | 205 | Psalm 94 | 251 |
| Psalm 50 | 206 | Psalm 95 | 252 |
| Psalm 51 | 208 | Psalm 96 | 253 |
| Psalm 52 | 209 | Psalm 97 | 254 |
| Psalm 53 | 210 | Psalm 98 | 255 |
| Psalm 54 | 211 | Psalm 99 | 256 |
| Psalm 55 | 212 | Psalm 100 | 257 |
| Psalm 56 | 213 | Psalm 101 | 258 |
| Psalm 57 | 214 | Psalm 102 | 259 |
| Psalm 58 | 215 | Psalm 103 | 260 |
| Psalm 59 | 216 | Psalm 104 | 261 |
| Psalm 60 | 217 | Psalm 105 | 262 |
| Psalm 61 | 218 | Psalm 106 | 263 |
| Psalm 62 | 219 | Psalm 107 | 264 |
| Psalm 63 | 220 | Psalm 108 | 265 |
| Psalm 64 | 221 | Psalm 109 | 266 |
| Psalm 65 | 222 | Psalm 110 | 267 |
| Psalm 66 | 223 | Psalm 111 | 268 |
| Psalm 67 | 224 | Psalm 112 | 269 |
| Psalm 68 | 225 | Psalm 113 | 270 |
| Psalm 69 | 226 | Psalm 114 | 271 |
| Psalm 70 | 227 | Psalm 115 | 272 |
| Psalm 71 | 228 | Psalm 116 | 273 |
| Psalm 72 | 229 | Psalm 117 | 274 |
| Psalm 73 | 230 | Psalm 118 | 275 |
| Psalm 74 | 231 | Psalm 119 | 276 |
| Psalm 75 | 232 | Psalm 120 | 277 |
| Psalm 76 | 234 | Psalm 121 | 278 |
| Psalm 77 | 235 | Psalm 122 | 279 |
| Psalm 78 | 236 | Psalm 123 | 280 |
| Psalm 79 | 236 | Psalm 124 | 281 |
| Psalm 80 | 237 | Psalm 125 | 282 |
| Psalm 81 | 238 | Psalm 126 | 283 |
| Psalm 82 | 239 | Psalm 127 | 284 |
| Psalm 83 | 240 | Psalm 128 | 285 |
| Psalm 84 | 241 | Psalm 129 | 286 |
| Psalm 85 | 242 | Psalm 130 | 287 |
| Psalm 86 | 243 | Psalm 131 | 288 |
| Psalm 87 | 244 | Psalm 132 | 289 |

| Reference | Page |
|---|---|
| Psalm 133 | 290 |
| Psalm 134 | 291 |
| Psalm 135 | 292 |
| Psalm 136 | 293 |
| Psalm 137 | 294 |
| Psalm 138 | 295 |
| Psalm 139 | 296 |
| Psalm 140 | 297 |
| Psalm 141 | 298 |
| Psalm 142 | 299 |
| Psalm 143 | 301 |
| Psalm 144 | 302 |
| Psalm 145 | 303 |
| Psalm 146 | 304 |
| Psalm 147 | 305 |
| Psalm 148 | 306 |
| Psalm 149 | 307 |
| Psalm 150 | 308 |
| Habakkuk 2:2—3 | 309 |
| Matthew 5:3 | 310 |
| Matthew 5:4 | 311 |
| Matthew 5:5 | 312 |
| Matthew 5:6 | 313 |
| Matthew 5:7 | 314 |
| Matthew 5:8 | 315 |
| Matthew 5:9 | 316 |
| Matthew 5:10 | 317 |
| Matthew 5:11—12 | 318 |
| Matthew 5:46 | 319 |
| Matthew 6:9—13 | 320 |
| Matthew 6:16—18 | 321 |
| Luke 22:31—32 | 322 |
| Luke 22:34 | 323 |
| Luke 22:41 | 324 |
| John 5:8 | 325 |
| Acts 9:4—6 | 326 |
| Acts 9:20—21 | 327 |
| Acts 9:22 | 328 |
| Romans 8:27 | 329 |
| Romans 8:29—30 | 330 |
| Romans 8:35 | 331 |
| Romans 8:37 | 332 |
| Romans 8:38—39 | 333 |
| 1 Corinthians 13:1 | 334 |
| 1 Corinthians 13:2 | 335 |
| 1 Corinthians 13:3 | 336 |
| 1 Corinthians 13:4 | 337 |
| 1 Corinthians 13:5 | 338 |
| 1 Corinthians 13:6 | 339 |
| 1 Corinthians 13:7 | 340 |
| 1 Corinthians 13:8 | 341 |
| 1 Corinthians 13:9 | 342 |
| 1 Corinthians 13:10 | 343 |
| 1 Corinthians 13:11 | 344 |
| 1 Corinthians 13:12 | 345 |
| 1 Corinthians 13:13 | 346 |
| Galatians 1:6—7 | 347 |
| Galatians 1:11—12 | 348 |
| Galatians 1:13—16 | 349 |
| Ephesians 3:14 | 350 |
| Ephesians 3:15 | 351 |
| Ephesians 3:16 | 352 |
| Ephesians 3:17 | 353 |
| Ephesians 3:18 | 354 |
| Ephesians 3:19 | 355 |
| Ephesians 3:20 | 356 |
| Ephesians 3:21 | 357 |
| Ephesians 4:1 | 358 |
| Ephesians 4:2 | 359 |
| Ephesians 4:3 | 360 |
| Ephesians 4:4—6 | 361 |
| Ephesians 4:11—13 | 362 |
| Ephesians 4:17—19 | 363 |
| Ephesians 4:20—22 | 364 |
| Ephesians 6:10 | 365 |
| Ephesians 6:11 | 366 |
| Ephesians 6:12 | 367 |
| Ephesians 6:13 | 368 |
| Ephesians 6:14 | 369 |
| Ephesians 6:15 | 370 |
| Ephesians 6:16 | 371 |
| Ephesians 6:17 | 372 |
| Ephesians 6:18 | 373 |
| Ephesians 6:19—20 | 374 |
| Titus 2:1—2 | 375 |
| Titus 2:3—5 | 376 |
| Titus 2:6—8 | 377 |
| Hebrews 11:3 | 378 |
| Hebrews 11:4 | 379 |
| Hebrews 11:5 | 380 |

| | | | |
|---|---|---|---|
| Hebrews 11:6 | 381 | Hebrews 11:17—18 | 388 |
| Hebrews 11:7 | 382 | Hebrews 11:21 | 389 |
| Hebrews 11:8 | 383 | Hebrews 11:39—40 | 390 |
| Hebrews 11:9 | 384 | Hebrews 12:1—3 | 391 |
| Hebrews 11:10 | 385 | 3 John 2 | 392 |
| Hebrews 11:11 | 386 | 3 John 3—4 | 393 |
| Hebrews 11:12 | 387 | | |

# ACKNOWLEDGEMENTS

God, thank You for Your plans for me. Thank You for **On This Journey Volume 2** and choosing me to complete Your project. **OTJ** has brought me to the next level. I just want to please You. Thank You for continuing to anoint me and to invest in me and my gifts, which keep surprising me. Thank You for loving and forgiving me.

Hillary, and Nehemiah, thank you for enduring my late nights, your ideas, the sounding board, the love and the support. Thank you for loving me, especially when I do nothing without a pen and a clipboard.

To my inner circle: keep me in your prayers. As one of you asked: "how do you match 2001-2002?" I responded you ask God. You know I have asked God for much, so for me, much is expected.

To my guardian children: Myya and Myles Malone. May these words touch your life and may you be able to see God in all that you do.

## About the Teacher

Minister Onedia N. Gage believes in the study of God's word. She wants youth to have the help she wanted and needed as a former youth so that you can grow with God. She hopes that you will seek God for a closer relationship so that you can have a closer relationship with your family and friends.

Her life philosophy is three – fold:
A) "What have you done today to invest in your future?"
B) Reading is essential to your positive contribution to our community; and,
C) "If not me, who? If not now, when?" She feels her time is best spent when youth benefit from her experiences.

Minister Onedia invites you to share her study at her youth retreat and upcoming conferences. Minister Onedia would like to pray for and with you. Please contact her via email onediagage@onediagage.com Via twitter @onediangage, on facebook.com/onedia-gage-ministries and phone 281-740-5143 or 512-715-GAGE (4243).

# Preacher ♦ Prayer Warrior ♦ Teacher

To invite Rev. Gage to preach, coach, teach, and pray, Please contact us at
@onediangage (twitter) ♦ onediagage@onediagage.com ♦
facebook.com/onediagage
youtube.com/onediagage ♦ blogtalkradio.com/onediagage ♦
www.onediagage.com

## Publishing

Do you have a book you want to write, but do not know what to do?

Do you have a book you need to publish but do not know how to start?

Would publishing move your career forward?

Let us help

onediagage@purpleink.net ♦ www.purpleink.net

713.705.5530

512.715.4243

www.ingramcontent.com/pod-product-compliance
Lightning Source LLC
Chambersburg PA
CBHW081738100526
44592CB00015B/2229